TEST YOURSELF offers in a single volume a wonderful collection of intelligence tests designed especially to be used in the privacy of your own home.

This book lets you take advantage of testing methods as used by leading psychological bureaux – industrial organisations – colleges – government departments. Each fascinating self-test is entertaining, yet deeply revealing.

Above all, TEST YOURSELF supplies you with a rich mine of practical information for use in your daily life and in furthering your career.

So, if you are not afraid of challenge – TEST YOURSELF! It will give you new insight into your abilities . . .

William Bernard
and Jules Leopold

Test Yourself

TEST YOURSELF

A CORGI BOOK   0 552 07200 1

Originally published in Great Britain by
Souvenir Press Ltd.

PRINTING HISTORY

Souvenir press edition published 1964
Corgi edition published 1965
Corgi edition reprinted 1967
Corgi edition reprinted 1968
Corgi edition reprinted 1969
Corgi edition reprinted 1970
Corgi edition reprinted 1972
Corgi edition reprinted 1973
Corgi edition reprinted 1975
Corgi edition reissued 1977
Corgi edition reprinted 1979
Corgi edition reprinted 1981
Corgi edition reprinted 1983
Corgi edition reprinted 1984
Corgi edition reprinted 1985
Corgi edition reprinted 1986
Corgi edition reprinted 1987
Corgi edition reprinted 1988
Corgi edition reprinted 1989

This book is set in 9/11 Times

Corgi Books are published by Transworld Publishers Ltd.,
61–63 Uxbridge Road, Ealing, London W5 5SA,
in Australia by Transworld Publishers (Australia) Pty. Ltd.,
15–23 Helles Avenue, Moorebank, NSW 2170, and in New
Zealand by Transworld Publishers (N.Z.) Ltd., Cnr. Moselle
and Waipareira Avenues, Henderson, Auckland.

Printed and bound in Great Britain by
BPCC Hazell Books Ltd
Member of BPCC Ltd
Aylesbury, Bucks, England

CONTENTS

Section One: GENERAL INTELLIGENCE

Section Two: SKILLS AND TALENTS

Section Three: PERSONALITY

Section Four: JOB APTITUDES

TEST YOURSELF

Introduction

THESE challenging tests allow you to look at yourself through science-tinted glasses. You need no expensive equipment. You need no laboratory. Yet you can apply advanced psychological techniques to the measurement of your own skills, talents and personality.

But a warning is in order. Since each trial is of the self-administered kind—with yourself sole judge and jury—absolute honesty on your part is essential.

Don't jump the gun. Don't peek at the answers. Don't credit yourself with doubtful or unearned points. Any satisfaction you might get out of cutting corners would be the same as that of the fellow who cheats himself at solitaire.

Objectivity Maintained

TEST YOURSELF is the first popular test manual to use a genuinely scientific approach. You will gain an insight into the testing methods relied upon more and more by government agencies, universities, institutions and private industry throughout the United States.

Further, TEST YOURSELF is the first work of its kind to rule out questions of an introspective or subjective nature.

Even the apparent exceptions have a twist that carries them clear of the subjective class.

The trouble with the subjective question is that it asks you to make a judgment of yourself. It requires you to respond directly to such scale items as: "Do you consider yourself happy?"—"Do you love life?"—"Are you uncomfortable with women?"

Such questions continue to blight psychological tests today, particularly personality scales. Obviously any subjective query permits wishful thinking, rationalization and anticipation of the desired answer to affect the result. Bad enough in any test, they would be fatal to the self-administered type.

The elimination in TEST YOURSELF of both subjective scale items and subjective scoring is no reflection on your honesty. The fact is that pride ourselves as we may on possessing objective judgment, it is psychologically impossible to view ourselves without prejudice. Bound to result are distortions resembling the *halo effect*, known to all psychologists.

You will not find any such overt subjectivity tainting your scores in the tests that follow.

Concerning Your Score

Do not look upon these or any other tests as indicating absolutely whether you are "good" or "bad" in a particular direction. The most a test can give you is a clue to your standing in a group.

Your standing is indicated here by the scoring ladder at the close of every test. The ladder tells where your score places you— on a level with the percentage of adults who score highest in a standardized group, or among those who get a lower mark. Theoretically, the group represents the population at large.

Probable Error

Your score, of course, will be subject to the same vagaries of chance which affect all human works.

Psychometrists, however, use an interesting mathematical method to estimate the extent to which chance alone will vary a test score. The method consists of statistical calculation of what is termed *Probable Error*, or PE.

The PE of your score is of direct concern to you. It can be interpreted as telling you the number of points you may have lost or gained through the workings of pure chance.

The PE for most of the tests is listed in the Answer Section. In certain cases, it is omitted, since the test is of a type not permitting calculation of a significant PE.

Section One:

GENERAL INTELLIGENCE

1. What's Your I. Q.?

TODAY the expression "I. Q." is on everyone's lips, yet few understand what it means. Like *inferiority complex* and other psychological terms drifting into the language, this one has become solidly fixed in the American vocabulary—and like them is frequently misused.

For one thing, the I. Q.—short for *intelligence quotient*—is too often confused in the popular mind with mental age.

Part of this confusion arises because "mental age" is what an intelligence test is generally scored to indicate. But the mental age must be considered in relation to actual age in years and months if the I. Q. is to be determined.

Take a lad of six with a mental age of ten years. You'll admit his development is different from that of a fifteen-year-old whose mental age is also ten years. The I. Q. is simply a convenient device to show this difference.

Misleading the Public

Another common error regarding the I. Q. can be blamed on self-styled "psychologists" who should know better.

Via television, radio, books and syndicated newspaper features of wide circulation, these pseudo-experts release a flood of tests and quizzes with titles on this order:

What's Your Sports I. Q.?
I. Q. Department
Your Literary I. Q.
I. Q. Quiz Section
Current Events I. Q. Test

The public is misled because such tests measure attitudes or knowledge, if anything. This is exactly the opposite of what your true I. Q. probe seeks.

The fact that you don't read sports columns or may not have gone to college doesn't mean you are stupid. Intelligence is not a matter of acquired knowledge, of how much you know. It is a matter of your capacity to know. Similarly the I. Q., or intelligence quotient, is not a measure of what you have learned, but rather of your ability to learn.

It is a weakness of virtually all intelligence tests, of course, that to some extent they do rely on knowledge. The test given here, for example, assumes that you know how to read.

Knowledge and False Scores

Such assumptions may lead to false scores. On the other hand, psychological research since the time of Binet has pretty well established a relation between intelligence and certain forms of knowledge. Thus, reading comprehension and extent of vocabulary have been found to vary so closely with intelligence that often they are actually used as guides to intelligence—and with results surprisingly consistent. In the test which follows, for the sake of speed and convenience, a number of vocabularly questions are included. *This may lead to a distorted score if you are foreign-born, or in other ways subject to language difficulty.*

All questions have been carefully selected for validity and consistency. The examination shows a retest reliablity of .87, and in no case has failed to correlate at least .81 with Stanford-Binet, Kuhlmann, Terman and other Binet-type scales, including the Dominion (group) and the Wechsler Adult Intelligence Scales. Mental age equivalents given below were derived through statistical comparison of scores achieved by the same individuals on the tests mentioned and the one given here.

Designed for Adults

The test is intended primarily for adults. It will work at all only if the person who takes it is more than thirteen years old.

But in calculating adult I. Q. it is essential to know the age at which intelligence does become "adult"—reaches full maturity, in other words.

Psychologists vary in their estimates. At one time guesses ranged all the way from twelve or thirteen years to twenty-one years. At present, however, the best psychological information points to the years between fifteen and seventeen as the ones in which full mental growth is achieved.

For purposes of this test, the age of maximum development is fixed at fifteen and one-half years, or 186 months. The figure is an average derived from intelligence tests of recognized standing. The scaling is such that minor distortion may occur in the I.Q.'s scored by those under fifteen and one-half years of age. This is more than compensated for by the increased accuracy afforded persons above that age, for whom the test is intended.

Figuring Your I. Q.

In order to find your I.Q. after taking the test, proceed as follows:

1. By examining the table at the end of the test, locate the Mental Age equivalent to your test score.
2. IF YOU ARE YOUNGER THAN FIFTEEN AND ONE-HALF YEARS— divide the Mental Age by your own age in months. Carry your answer to two decimal places.
3. IF YOUR AGE IS FIFTEEN AND ONE-HALF YEARS OR MORE— divide the Mental Age by 186. Carry your answer to two decimal places.
4. Multiply your answer by 100. The resulting figure is your I.Q.

Here are two examples:

A person fourteen years and three months old scores 60 on the test (60 correct answers).

The table shows that 60 is equivalent to a Mental Age of 216. 216 divided by 171 (age in months) is equal to 1.26.

Multiplying by 100 yields 126—so the boy has an I. Q. of 126.

An adult forty-six years old scores 30 on the test. (30 correct answers.)

The table shows that 30 is equivalent to a Mental Age of 153.
153 divided by 186 is equal to .82.
Multiplying by 100 yields 82—so the adult has an I.Q. of 82.

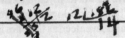

DIRECTIONS—In this test, work as fast as you can without sacrificing accuracy. If you wish, you may make calculations on the page margins or on a separate sheet of paper. Remember not to work too long on any one question; skip the hard ones and return to them later should you have time.

Each question is self-explaining. Here are some sample questions, with correct answers as you should write them.

91. MAN *is to* BOY *as* WOMAN *is to*
(1) lad (2) kid (3) dame (4) girl (5) crowd . . . . (*4*)

92. In this series, what number comes next?
2, 4, 6, 8, ... (*10*)

93. These words can be arranged to form a sentence. If the sentence is true, write T. If the sentence is false, write F.
ARE NEVER TREES GREEN . . . .(*F*)
(*The words can be arranged into the sentence* TREES ARE NEVER GREEN, *which is false.*)

94. In this group, which object does not belong?
(1) pencil (2) pen (3) crayon (4) brush (5) club . . . . . .(*5*)
(*You can draw or write with pencil, pen, crayon or brush, but not with a club.*)

Make sure to glance at a watch or clock occasionally; or better still, have someone time you. If you work longer than the time allowed, your score will be false. When you understand the sample questions, begin the test.

TIME LIMIT: 45 MINUTES

1. TRUMPET *is to* PLAY *as* BOOK *is to*
   (1) fun (2) read (3) music (4) words (5) relax........ (**2**)

2. AUTOMOBILE *is to* WHEEL *as* HORSE *is to*
   (1) leg (2) tail (3) gallop (4) wagon (5) drive........ (**1**)

3. In this series, what number comes next?
   3, 9, 15, 21, ... (**27**)

4. COW *is to* BARN *as* MAN *is to*
   (1) stable (2) milk (3) house (4) farm (5) restaurant.. (**3**)

5. 1, 2, 3, 4, 5, 6, 7, 8, 9, 10, 11, 12, 13, 14, 15, 16
   Which number is the seventh number after the number
   just before 6? .... (**12**)

6. These words can be arranged to form a sentence. If the
   sentence is true, write T. If the sentence is false, write F.
   BURN WOOD CAN'T DRY.................... (**F**)

7. These words can be arranged to form a sentence. If the
   sentence is true, write T. If the sentence is false, write F.
   ON FLOAT BOATS NEVER WATER.......... (**F**)

8. In this series, what number comes next?
   1, 3, 5, 7, ... (**9**)

9. These words can be arranged to form a sentence. If the
   sentence is true, write T. If the sentence is false, write F.
   A BAT PLAYED WITH BASEBALL IS .... (**T**)

10. NEGLIGENT means
    (1) careless (2) cautious (3) unimportant (4) careful.. (**1**)

11. John has 10 cents. If he had 3 cents less he would have
    half as much as George. George has how much more
    money than John?
    (a) 7 cents (b) 4 cents (c) 2 cents (d) 13 cents........ (**b**)

12. HE *is to* HIM *as* SHE *is to*
    (1) me (2) them (3) hers (4) her (5) his.............. (**4**)

13. In this group, which object does not belong?
    (1) radio (2) battery (3) boiler (4) telephone........ (**3**)

✶ 14. In this group, which object does not belong?
(1) saber (2) rapier (3) scimitar (4) lance (5) cutlass.. (**4**)

✓ 15. Only birds have feathers, therefore which is true?
(1) Birds shed in the spring.
(2) All feathers are light.
(3) Snakes don't have feathers .... (**3**)

✓ 16. In this group, which word does not belong?
(1) architect (2) builder (3) plumber (4) doctor ...... (**4**)

✓ 17. In this series, what number comes next?
90, 85, 75, 60, 40, ... (**5**)

✓ 18. In this series, what number comes next?
22, 33, 44, 55, 66, ... (**77**)

✗ 19. BOTANIST is to SOCIOLOGIST as PLANT is to
(1) women (2) problems (3) society (4) sociology.... ( )

✗ 20. If a person is DISTRAUGHT, he is
(1) ignorant (2) manic (3) shocked (4) bewildered.... (**3**)

✓ 21. THREAD is to CLOTH as WIRE is to
(1) stiff (2) radio (3) rope (4) mesh (5) metal........ (**4**)

✓ 22. SANITATION makes for
(1) water (2) health (3) porcelain (4) godliness...... (**2**)

✓ 23. In this series, what letter comes next?
A C E G I .... (**K**)

✗ 24. Which number is wrong in this series?
1, 19, 8, 5, 145, 127 .... ( )

✓ 25. Print the letter as far from the first letter of the alphabet as
the second I is from the first I in INHARMONIOUS (**J**)

✓ 26. Which letter does not belong in this series?
Z Y X Q W V .... (**Q**)

✗ 27.

..............(**d**)

18

28. These words can be arranged to form a sentence. If the sentence is true, write T. If the sentence is false, write F.
DESTROY BOMBING CITIES CAN'T AND MEN .... (F)

29. In this series, which number comes next?
18, 12, 15, 10, 12, 8, ? .... ( )

30. If A and B are letters write C, unless 5 and 5 add up to 10, in which case don't write anything but D. .... (D)

31. These words can be arranged to form a sentence. If the sentence is true, write T. If the sentence is false, write F.
TEETH NOT ARE FALSE TRUE TEETH ...... (T)

32.

(a) ...... (b) ...... (c) ...... (d) ...... (e) ...... (b)

33.

(a) ⊔ (b) ⊓ (c) E (d) Ǝ (e) ...... (d)

34. Which number is wrong in this series?
2, 6, 17, 54, 162, ... ( )

35. In this series, what letter comes next?
A C F J .... (O)

36.

(a) ...... (b) ...... (c) ...... (d) ...... (e) ...... (c)

19

√ 37. In this series, what number comes next?
21, 20, 18, 15, 11, ... (6)

√ 38. SOUTH is to NORTHWEST as WEST is to
(1) north (2) southwest (3) northeast (4) southeast.... (3)

✗ 39. In this series, which number does not belong?
2, 4, 100, 38, 20, 7, ... ( )

√ 40. In this group, which word does not belong?
(1) sadness (2) melancholy (3) sorrow (4) mourning.. (4)

√ 41. In this series, what letter comes next?
A C B D F E G . ... (I)

√ 42. 1, 2, 3, 4, 5, 6, 7, 8, 9, 10, 11, 12, 13, 14, 15, 16, 17, 18, 19
Print the number which comes as far before 14 in the
series above as K comes after F in the alphabet...... (9)

✗ 43. If all men have coats, then big men have
(1) big coats (2) fewer coats (3) coats (4) few coats.... ( )

√ 44. In this series, what number comes next?
18, 24, 21, 27, 24, 30, 27 .... ( )

✗ 45. Nazis PLUNDERED cities by
(1) guns (2) arson (3) destroying them (4) robbing them
(5) knocking them down .... (3)

√ 46. In this series, what number comes next?
66, 63, 57, 45, ... (21)

✗ 47.

(a) □ (b) ● (c) ■ (d) ▣ (e) ○ ..( )

✗ 48. In this series, what number comes next?
2, 9, 6, 7, 18, 5, ... ( )

✗ 49. PLANE is to SOLID as LINE is to
(1) square (2) circle (3) angle (4) rectangle (5) plane.. (5)

√ 50. How many miles can a dog run in 3 minutes if it runs half
as fast as a car going 40 miles per hour?.............. (I)

20

51. A canoe always has (1) paddles (2) canvas (3) water (4) paint (5) length................................. (5)

52. In this series what number comes next?
65, 68, 72, 77, 83, ... **90** ..... ( )

53. How many letters in this line fall next to vowels but after K or R?
PAULEGKATLOIRQOZ................. (1)

54. In this series what number comes next?
2, A, 9, B, 6, C, 13, D,........................... ( )

55. How many letters in the line below come after the K, but both before R and after T?
AABKMXJTTVCRRPL.................... (4)

56. 20 men can dig 40 holes in 60 days so 10 men can dig 20 holes in how many days?.......................... (60)

57. How many letters in this series come just before an odd number and just after a number larger than 6?
Z, 1, 9, A, 4, B, 3, 14, 19, C, 8, 9, B, 5, D, 12, E, 17.... (2)

58. Suppose Milwaukee leads the league and Pittsburgh is fifth, while St. Louis is midway between them. If Chicago is ahead of Pittsburgh and Cincinnati is immediately behind St. Louis, which city is in second place?
(a) Cincinnati (b) Pittsburgh (c) Chicago (d) St. Louis (e) Milwaukee .... (c)

59. One series below is in opposite order to the other, except for a certain number. Write the number.
1, 2, 3   1, 3, 2 .... (1)

60. COMPREHENSIBLE advice is
(1) bad advice (2) comprehensive (3) understandable (4) good advice (5) reprehensible.................. (3)

61. In this group, which word does not belong?
(1) the (2) this (3) an (4) it (5) a..................... (4)

62. Which of these words comes closest in meaning to IS?
(1) to be (2) are (3) lives (4) exists (5) accrusticates.... (1)

21

63. A CHASSEUR is a (1) soldier (2) torso (3) detective (4) vase .... ( )

64. BLEAK *is to* BLACK *as* LEAK *is to*
(1) white (2) back (3) leak (4) lack (5) water .... (4)

65. ADAMANT is the opposite of
(1) dull (2) unlike Adam (3) yielding (4) stubborn.... (3)

66. Half a waiter's earnings, and a dollar besides, come from tips. If he earns 15 dollars, how many dollars come from tips? .... 4:5 .... (5)

67. Which of these words most nearly corresponds in meaning to OPULENT?
(1) exposed (2) precious stone (3) wealthy (4) exposed at one end (5) weeping............................... (3)

68. If a train is running 3 minutes late and losing 3 seconds per minute, how many more minutes will it take for the train to be running an hour late?....................( )

69. Which of these words most nearly corresponds in meaning to DELETE?
(1) permit (2) erase (3) rent (4) tasty (5) neat .... (2)

70. Girls always have (1) sweethearts (2) clothes (3) giggles (4) hair (5) figures .... (4)

71. A train running 30 miles per hour is in front of a train running 50 miles per hour. How many miles apart are the trains, if it will take 15 minutes for the faster train to catch the slower one? .... ( )

72. PIQUE is most similar in meaning to
(1) choice (2) decoration (3) elf (4) resentment (5) sorrow .... (4)

73. A train completes half a trip at 30 miles per hour, and the other half at 60 miles per hour. If the whole trip was 20 miles, how many minutes did the train take to complete the trip? .... ( )

74. Print your answer. A B D *is to* C B A *as* Q R T *is to*...... ( )

75. If 2 is A and 6 is C and 8 is D and 12 is F, how would you spell BEADED, using numbers instead of letters?...... ( )

4 10 2 8 10 4

76. When Aunt Carrie makes soup, she puts in 1 bean for each 2 peas. If her soup contains a total of 300 peas and beans, how many peas are there?...**200**............( )

77. No dog can sing, but some dogs can talk. If so, then
   (1) Some dogs can sing.
   (2) All dogs can't sing.
   (3) All dogs can't talk ....**2**..........( )

78. No man is good, but some men are not bad. Therefore,
   (1) All men are not bad.
   (2) No man is not bad.
   (3) All men aren't good .....**3**.................( )

79. The Potomac River and the Hudson River have a combined length of 850 miles, and the Hudson River is 250 miles shorter than the Potomac River. How many miles long is the Potomac River? ......**300 550**......( )

80. Smith and Jones went to the race track, where Smith lost 68 dollars on the first 2 races, losing 6 dollars more on the second race than he lost on the first one. But he lost 4 dollars less on the second race than Jones did. How much did Jones lose on the second race? ....( )

81. Stockings always have
   (1) sexiness (2) seams (3) garters (4) weight
   (5) sheerness..................**4**..........( )

82. In this series, what number comes next?
   9, 7, 8, 6, 7, 5, ..**6**..............................( )

83. One bunch of bananas has one-third again as many bananas as a second bunch. If the second bunch has 3 less bananas than the first bunch, how many has the first bunch? ....( )

84.

85. Birds can only fly and hop, but worms can crawl. Therefore,
    (1) Birds eat worms.
    (2) Birds don't crawl.
    (3) Birds sometimes crawl ..... *2* .... ( )

86. Boxes always have (1) angles (2) shapes (3) wood (4) string ....*1*....................... ( )

87. What number is as much more than 10 as it is less than one-half of what 30 is 10 less than? .... ( )

88. Smith gets twice as large a share of the profits as any of his three partners gets. The three partners share equally. What fraction of the entire profits is Smith's?. *2/5* .... ( )

89. BIRD is to FISH as AIRPLANE is to
    (1) boat (2) whale (3) dory (4) ship (5) submarine .... *(5)*

90. These words can be arranged to form a sentence. If the sentence is true, write T. If the sentence is false, write F.
    ONE IN IS NUMBER THAN MORE BOOKS BOOK... *(T)*

TABLE OF MENTAL AGES (IN MONTHS)

YOUR SCORE	YOUR MENTAL AGE	YOUR SCORE	YOUR MENTAL AGE	YOUR SCORE	YOUR MENTAL AGE
2	94	32	157	61	218
3	96	33	159	62	221
4	98	34	162	63	223
5	100	35	164	64	225
6	103	36	166	65	227
7	105	37	168	66	229
8	107	38	170	67	231
9	109	39	172	68	233
10	111	40	174	69	235
11	113	41	176	70	237
12	115	42	178	71	240
13	117	43	181	72	242
14	119	44	183	73	244
15	122	45	185	74	246
16	124	46	187	75	248
17	126	47	189	76	250
18	128	48	191	77	252
19	130	49	193	78	254
20	132	50	195	79	256
21	134	51	197	80	259
22	136	52	199	81	261
23	138	53	202	82	263
24	140	54	204	83	265
25	143	55	206	84	267
26	145	56	208	85	269
27	147	57	210	86	271
28	149	58	212	87	273
29	151	59	214	88	275
30	153	60	216	89	278
31	155				

Your I. Q. . . . .
Average I. Q.: 101

SUPERIOR	(UPPER ONE PER CENT)	Above 140
EXCELLENT	(NEXT THREE PER CENT)	131–140
GOOD	(NEXT TWENTY-SIX PER CENT)	111–130
NORMAL	(NEXT FORTY-TWO PER CENT)	91–110
DULL	(NEXT TWENTY-FOUR PER CENT)	71–90
INFERIOR	(LOWEST FOUR PER CENT)	Below 71

2. Are You Adaptable?

SOME authorities lean toward the idea that intelligence is the capacity to learn. Others believe it is the ability to solve problems. Still others define intelligence as *adaptability*—the capacity for adjusting to the particular circumstances in which a man finds himself.

There is even a large school of thought, quite as sound as any other, which holds that intelligence includes bodily strength, speed of reflex and similar "physical" characteristics. For, asks this school, if intelligence is adaptability, does not the stronger, swifter person generally adapt himself better than the slower, weaker one?

Contradictions Only Apparent

The intelligence guides in this book, however, do not bother with the functions of your body below the neck. Because in the end it is the functioning at brain level that makes for greatest adaptability. True, a man has not the claws of a lion. But he does not try to scratch a lion to death. He invents a rifle.

All agree that this is adaptability. All agree that this is intelligence—even though differences may exist concerning its exact meaning.

Actually, there is less contradiction among definitions than might appear at first glance. Thus, learning capacity means essentially the capacity to learn *to solve problems*. A parrot can learn by rote to recite numbers. But it cannot learn to solve the problem, say, of counting the people in a room—so it is less "intelligent" than you are.

Likewise with adaptability. *Adapting* to an environment can be interpreted to mean *solving the problems* presented by that environment.

Detecting Relationships Important

Going further into the question of adaptability, psychologists have learned that to a large extent it involves the discerning of relationships. Out of your own experience, you know that when you walk into a new situation it presents you with new problems; and the quicker you are to discover their elements and how these relate to each other, the quicker you are to solve those problems.

The type of question given here formed part of the general I. Q. quiz (*Test I*). If your I. Q. score disappointed you, this test may tell you why. The elements in each line represent a series—that is, a definite relationship can be found to exist among them. How good are you at detecting the relationships, at sizing up the situations?

DIRECTIONS—The figures in every line follow some definite sequence. Fill in the blank space with the figure which should come next. For example: 13, 11, 9, 7, 5 represent a sequence whose next figure would be 3.

TIME LIMIT: 10 MINUTES

√1. 20, 17, 14, 11, ...8...............

√2. 16, 15, 13, 12, 10, 9, 7...............

√3. H g F e D c B...............

√4. 3, 8, 5, 10, 7, 12...............

√5. J L N P R T................

√6. A A C B B D C..................

√7. 1, 3, 9, 27, ...81................

√8. 47, 38, 30, 23, 17, 12............

√9.

27

10. 5, 6, 4, 7, 3, 8, *2* ....

11. a C B d F E g *H* ....

12. / // /// //// ///// ///// //   ...*/*......

13. (figures)   ...(drawing)......

14. 10, 8, 16, 13, 39, 35, ...

15. A Z Y B X W *C* ....

16. 26, 20, 4, 16, 10, 2, 14, ...

17. * ** *** **** *** ** *(star)* ....

18. * **** ** **** *** ....

19. 30, 15, 45, 15, 60, *15* ....

20. A B D G K P *✓* ....

21. (squares)   ...(drawing)......

22. (circles/faces)   ...(drawing)......

23. (wheels)   ...*O*......

24. 1, Z, 3, X, 4, *W* ....

25. 2, B, 4, D, 6, *F* ....

26. 1, 10, 2, 9, 3, *8* ....

27. M L N K O J *P* ....

28

28. 24, 15, 9, 6, .. 6 ....

29. b Y d W F ....

30. C e C E g E G ....

Your Score . . . . .
Average Score : 48
SUPERIOR (UPPER TEN PER CENT)   69–90
GOOD (NEXT TWENTY PER CENT)   57–66
FAIR   (NEXT THIRTY PER CENT)   48–54
POOR (LOWEST FORTY PER CENT)   0–45

29

3. Do You Really See?

BOTH "learning capacity" and "the ability to solve problems" have certain advantages as definitions of intelligence. They tend to eliminate contradictions arising from the use of "adaptability" alone as a criterion.

The fellow with the gray matter, for one thing, may not always be the most adaptable in a particular situation. Work with mental and aptitude tests has shown that intelligence often goes hand in hand with distaste for routine tasks—and so may be a handicap, rather than a help, in some walks of life.

As if you didn't know! How many clever persons among your friends would be happy or expert if working, say, as dishwashers?

Two Sides to the Story

But the evidence is not all in. On the contrary side, take just these two instances:

1. *Comparatively intelligent dogs, rather than stupid ones, are the last to crack up in the laboratory under strains simulating those of our civilization.* (Frustration, continuous necessity for decision, etc.)

2. *Despite popular belief, in both World Wars and the Korean War the high I. Q. soldiers succumbed to shell shock or battle fatigue less often than low I. Q. men under like conditions.*

Such clues indicate that intelligence still has by no means been disqualified as the essence of human adaptability. Yes, evidence exists to the effect that your smart fellow is less able to get by under certain conditions—because of emotional or other stresses that go with the high-powered brain. The point is that he is likely to get by under a *wider variety* of conditions—in more environments —although he may fail in any particular one.

An earthworm can survive with a couple of feet of dirt in its face, and man cannot. But man can live for periods at the North Pole, under the sea, in the sky, even miles underground—all places where the worm would die, since it hasn't the brain with which to adapt itself.

Perception Is Initial Step

This brings us to perception, without which there can be no learning, no solving of problems. Perception is the first move in the whole adaptive process. If you cannot *perceive* the characteristics of your environment, your efforts to adapt yourself can only be purely random—like those of a man deprived of senses, unable to tell night from day, heat from cold.

We assume that you can make such gross perceptions; that all your senses are in fair working order. But how good are you at perceiving things with your brain?

This test gives you a chance to find out.

After completing Part One, rest at least five minutes before starting Part Two.

Part One:
DIRECTIONS—Examine the sample row of figures on the next page. You will notice that the first and fifth figures are virtually alike. Check these figures with your pencil.

Similarly, in each of the numbered rows are two figures which are virtually alike. Check these figures.

TIME LIMIT: 1 MINUTE

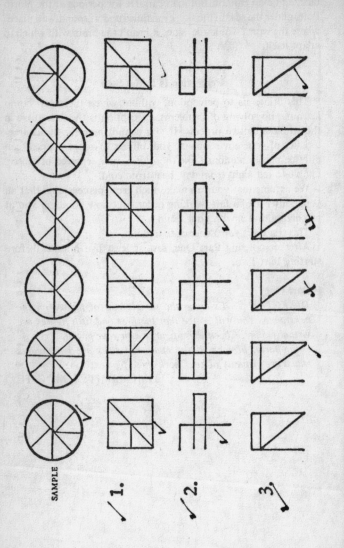

SAMPLE

1.

2.

3.

32

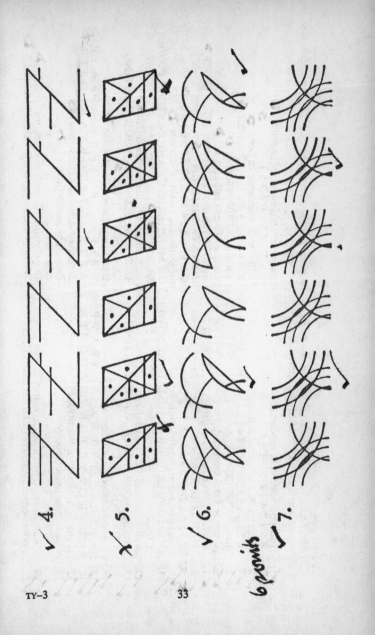

4.

5.

6.

group 6

7.

Part Two:

DIRECTIONS—On each line there are two items. If the items are the same, mark S. If the items show any difference, mark D. TIME LIMIT: 3 MINUTES.

1. ..pschyozoatechnimonochromite
2. ..8 6 2 7 4 1 8 0 6 3 5 1
3. ..Charles B. Fortescue & Sons
4. ..8 7 5 6 4 5 3 7 0 9 8 5 7 4 3 2 2
5. ..b46dhet78f7f0f9f8lkrjht
6. ..Gunnar Gael Galbaird, Jr.
7. ..agt......56,q.......oaglips......1496321
8. ..HEXATRIXIMENIA
9. ..2 3 5 5 6 5 4 5 5 3 5 7 5 8 5 6 3 8 2
10. ..agglutinated tintinabulation
11. ..HEMISPHERIC URANIUMATING POWER CORP.
12. ..aaiuuuiiauuiaiiiaiuiaiiaaiuua
13. ..INCH PIPELINING AGGRANDITING COMPANY, INC.
14. ..tetrahydrobetanapthaylamine
15. ..APTR.....PYTRA.....TRAYP
16. ..ARTRCRYRTORYRAGQPTR
17. ..Jonathan Algernon Pensitrone
18. ..2acetophenoneorthooxy-quinoline
19. ..Brandywine, Goerck & Lars, Inc. & Son
20. ..WKopertszxxsjjshwbajsiIIIIITLLLLLLI

1. pschyozoatechnimonachromite
2. 8 6 2 7 4 1 8 0 6 3 5 1
3. Charles B. Fortescue & Sons
4. 8 7 5 6 4 5 3 7 0 9 8 5 7 4 3 2 2 5
5. b46dhet78f7f0f9f8ikrjht
6. Gunnar Gael Galbaird Jr.
7. agt......56,q.......oaglips......1496321
8. HEXATRIXIMENIA
9. 2 3 5 5 6 5 4 5 5 3 5 7 5 8 5 6 3 8 2
10. agglutinated tintinnabulation
11. HEMISPHERIC URANIUMATING POWER CORP.
12. aaiuuuiiauuiaiiiaiuiaiiaaiuua
13. INCH PIPELINING AGGRANDITING COMPANY, INC.
14. tetrahydrobetanapthaylamine
15. APTR.....PYTRA.....TRAYP S
16. ARTRCRYRTORYARGQPTR
17. Jonathan Algernon Penistrone
18. 2acetophenoneorthooxy-quinoline
19. Brandywine, Goerck & Lars, Inc. & Son
20. WKopertszxxsjjshwbajsiIIIIITLLLLLLI

34

Your Score . . . . .
Average Score : 35

✓ SUPERIOR (UPPER TEN PER CENT)   85–100
　　GOOD (NEXT TWENTY PER CENT)   78–84
　　FAIR　(NEXT THIRTY PER CENT)   71–77
　　POOR (LOWEST FORTY PER CENT)   0–33

4. Can You Concentrate?

ATTENTION is a primary component of intelligence, most psychologists agree; and concentration may be defined as *exclusive* attention. You know well enough that if you give your entire attention to a task—that is to say, if you concentrate on that task —you will perform it more accurately, and more quickly, than if you allow your attention to wander.

Strictly speaking, there is no such thing as entire attention, at least not for more than short periods. Laboratory results would seem to place the top limit of the attention span at 30 seconds or less, although some estimates go as high as 90 seconds. Beyond this length of time, attention momentarily digresses, to be brought back to the task in hand by the process called "concentration."

We are all familiar with the way sunbeams can ignite a fire if focused through a lens. Similarly, your energies can turn out a better job if focused on the problem confronting you. The intelligent mind is one which can avoid distractions and concentrate on essentials.

Here is a test of your concentration. You are asked to examine a mass of numerals, focusing your mind wholly on locating certain pairs. Since this is a speed test, if you are distracted by the remaining numerals it will affect your rate and so show in your score.

DIRECTIONS—In each line are pairs of adjoining figures which add up to 10. Find them and underline them. For example:

Z: 2 9 4 6 1 1 9 3 5 5 6 7 8 5 4 7

Work as rapidly as you can. Be careful not to exceed the time limit or your score will be false

TIME LIMIT: 7 MINUTES

SUPERIOR .. 0-26 (Upper 10%)

GOOD ....27-37 (Next 20%)

FAIR ...... 38-48 (Next 30%)

POOR .... 49-143 (Lowest 40%)

Your Score ....

Average Score: 45

A:
B:
C:
D:
E:
F:
G:
H:
I:
J:
K:
L:
M:
N:
O:
P:
Q:
R:
S:
T:
U:
V:
W:
X:
Y:

37

5. How's Your Memory?

ONE inferiority makes another. If your attention is poor, this tends to weaken perception and memory both. The ray of hope is that such faculties often can be strengthened by cultivation. So if you don't do too well on the memory scales which follow, it might pay you to systematically practice the memorizing of words, objects, etc.

Further, weakness in one department can be covered up sometimes by strength in another. Suppose your perception is not so keen but your memory good; in that case you might score as well on a general mental test as someone, say, with good perception but poor memory.

In like fashion the man of medium intelligence but broad experience can sometimes solve the problems of life better than the highly intelligent man with little experience. The psychological reason for this is that retained experience provides the brain with more material to relate into a pattern of choices, and so makes it more likely that the choice will be a correct one.

Various Types of Memory

In judging intelligence we attempt to divorce it from experience. Memory, or retention, is therefore open to criticism as a component; it may properly belong at the sensory level. The memory expert, you'll agree, is not necessarily intelligent.

Yet obviously memory is an essential part of the learning process. And the capacity to retain experience—quite apart from the extent of such experience—if not part of adaptability, is at least potential to it.

38

Memory can be divided into types according to the varieties of image retained; you remember what you hear, see, touch, taste, feel. Visual retention lends itself best to self-administered tests of the kind in this book. Two tests follow. Be sure to take them at least a half-hour apart.

Part One:
DIRECTIONS—Study the words on the next page for exactly 2 minutes, writing them down on the blank lines if you think this will help you to remember. Then turn back to this page and on the numbered lines below write as many words as you can recall.

1. liberty
2. Money
3. sun
4. for,
5. bird
6. dress
7. wool
8. shoe
9. button
10. ring
11. America
12. people
13. photography
14. psychology
15. color
16. head
17. science
18.
19.
20.

1. Liberty ....
2. people ....
3. saw ....
4. Bird ....
5. for ....
6. glue ....
7. America ....
8. Dress ....
9. Psychology ......
10. Money ....

11. Ring ....
12. Front ....
13. Head ....
14. Color ....
15. Modern ....
16. Shoes ....
17. wool ....
18. photography ....
19. Button ....
20. science ....

Part Two:
DIRECTIONS—Inspect the diagrams in the dark area for exactly 2 minutes. Then cover them with your hand, and see how many you can reproduce with your pencil in the space below them. You can reproduce them in any order.

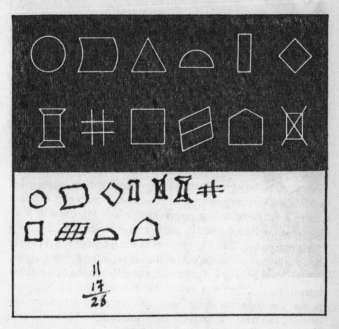

6. Do you think Straight?

DESPITE painstaking investigation, uncertainty remains concerning just which ingredients make up the mixture of abilities we call *intelligence*. But you don't have to be a psychologist to know that reasoning power—like flour in a cake recipe—is the important element in the blend.

Your ability to reason, actually, is your ability to make use of what your senses tell you. It is therefore a stage beyond other probable factors of intelligence such as attention—perception—memory. These alone cannot make you act intelligently. At best they merely *help* you to do so—by taking part in passing on, sorting and retaining information absorbed by your eyes and ears.

But it is the reasoning power itself which integrates this information, relates it piece by piece, makes patterns of it; it is the reasoning power, in short, which gives you a chance to act to your best advantage under the circumstances reported by your senses.

Speed and accuracy of inference, according to the best psychological studies, yields a rather reliable measure of reasoning power. The questions which follow give you a chance to show how well you can reason by the inferential method.

DIRECTIONS—Each set of statements is followed by one or more conclusions. You are to assume that the statements are correct. Any conclusion you consider true and logical according to the statements, mark T. Any conclusion you consider not necessarily true according to the statements, mark F. Mark ALL conclusions either T or F. For example:

A. I am taller than John. John is taller than Joe. Therefore:

1 . . T . . I am taller than Joe.

    B. My brother plays on a baseball team. Baseball teams have pitchers. Therefore:

    1 . . F . . My brother is a pitcher.

C. If the stars shine tonight, tomorrow's weather will be warm. The stars do shine tonight. Therefore:

1..F..Tomorrow's weather will not be warm.

2..F..The stars will shine tomorrow night.

3..T..Tomorrow's weather will be warm.

Now begin the test. Work accurately.

TIME LIMIT: 20 MINUTES.

---

1. Elephants are animals. Animals have legs. Therefore:

1....Elephants have legs. **T**

2. My secretary isn't old enough to vote. My secretary has beautiful hair. Therefore:

1....My secretary is a girl under 21 years of age. **F**

3. Few stores on this street have neon lights, but they all have awnings. Therefore:

1....Some have either awnings or neon lights. **F**

2....Some have both awnings and neon lights. **T**

4. All zublets have 3 eyes. This keptick has 3 eyes. Therefore:

1....This keptik is the same as a zublet. **F**

5. Potatoes are cheaper than tomatoes. I don't have enough money to buy two pounds of potatoes. Therefore:

1....I haven't enough money to buy a pound of tomatoes. **T**

2....I may or may not have enough money to buy a pound of tomatoes. **T**

6. Willie Mays is as good a hitter as Stan Musial. Stan Musial is a better hitter than most. Therefore:

1....Willie Mays should lead the league. **F**

2....Stan Musial should lead the league, especially in home runs. **F**

3....Willie Mays is a better hitter than most. **T**

43

7. Good musicians play classical music. You have to practice to be a good musician. Therefore:

✓ 1. . . . *Classical music requires more practice than jazz.* ☛

8. If your child is spoiled, spanking him will make him angry. If he is not spoiled, spanking him will make you sorry. But he is either spoiled or not spoiled. Therefore:

✓ 1. . . . *Spanking him will either make you sorry or make him angry.* ☜

✗ 2. . . . *It may not do any good to spank him.* ☜

9. Squares are shapes with angles. This shape has no angles. Therefore:

✓ 1. . . . *This shape is a circle.* ☛

✗ 2. . . . *Any conclusion is uncertain.* ☜

✓ 3. . . . *This shape is not a square.* ☜

10. Greenville is northeast of Smithtown. New York is northeast of Smithtown. Therefore:

✓ 1. . . . *New York is closer to Greenville than to Smithtown.* ☛

✓ 2. . . . *Smithtown is southwest of New York.* ☜

✓ 3. . . . *New York is near Smithtown.* ☝

11. If green is heavy, red is light. If yellow is light, blue is medium. But green is heavy, or yellow is light. Therefore:

✗ 1. . . . *Blue is medium.* ☜

✗ 2. . . . *Yellow and red are light.* ☜

✗ 3. . . . *Red is light, or blue is medium.* ☛

12. You are in your car, and if you stop short you will be hit by a truck behind you. If you don't stop short, you will hit a woman crossing the road. Therefore:

✓ 1. . . . *Pedestrians should keep off the roads.* ☝

✓ 2. . . . *The truck is going too fast.* ☝

✓ 3. . . . *You will be hit by the truck, or you will hit the woman.* ☜

13. I live between Joe's farm and the city. Joe's farm is between the city and the airport. Therefore:

1....Joe's farm is nearer to where I live than to the airport.

2....I live between Joe's farm and the airport.

3....I live nearer to Joe's farm than to the airport.

14. A wise gambler never takes a chance unless the odds are in his favor. A good gambler never takes a chance unless he has much to gain. This gambler takes a chance sometimes. Therefore:

1....He is either a good gambler or a wise one.

2....He may or may not be a good gambler.

3....He is neither a good gambler nor a wise one.

15. When B is Y, A is Z. E is either Y or Z, when A is not Z. Therefore:

1....When B is Y, E is neither Y nor Z.

2....When A is Z, Y or Z is E.

3....When B is not Y, E is neither Y nor Z.

16. When B is larger than C, X is smaller than C. But C is never larger than B. Therefore:

1....X is never larger than B.

2....X is never smaller than B.

3....X is never smaller than C.

17. As long as red is X, green must be Y. As long as green is not Y, blue must be Z. But blue is never Z when red is X. Therefore:

1....As long as blue is Z, green can be Y.

2....As long as red is not X, blue need not be Z.

3....As long as green is not Y, red cannot be X.

18. Indians are sometimes Alaskans. Alaskans are sometimes lawyers. Therefore:

1....Indians are not necessarily sometimes Alaskan lawyers.

2....Indians can't be Alaskan lawyers.

19. Going ahead would not mean death without dishonor, but going backward would not mean dishonor without death. Therefore:

✓ 1 .... *Going backward would mean death without dishonor.* F

✓ 2 .... *Going ahead could mean dishonor without death.* ✗

✗ 3 .... *Going ahead could mean death without dishonor.* T

20. B platoon attacked the enemy and was wiped out, maybe. Smith, a member of B platoon, recovered in base hospital. Therefore:

✗ 1 .... *The rest of B platoon was wiped out.* T

✓ 2 .... *All of B platoon was wiped out.* ✗

✓ 3 .... *All of B platoon was not wiped out.* T

Your Score .....
Average Score: 23

SUPERIOR (UPPER TEN PER CENT)   0–13

GOOD (NEXT TWENTY PER CENT)   14–19

FAIR   (NEXT THIRTY PER CENT)   20–25

POOR (LOWEST FORTY PER CENT)   26–48

7. How Smart Are You?

AGAIN on the subject of reasoning power—looked at in another way it boils down to the ability to solve problems by use of the brain; and this, as we have seen, may be the whole story of intelligence.

At any rate, it is the proof of the pudding. We may be led to call a person "smart" because of his quick attention, deep perception, showy memory. Still we change our minds quickly enough if these fail to bring that person to logical conclusions and right answers.

The reasoning power has already been tested by grading your skill at inference. Here we measure it by rating your facility at direct problem solving. Of course, problems occur in all the tests in this book; every test is itself a problem. But here and in the preceding quiz the questions are weighted and scaled so that differences in scores will indicate primarily differences in the reasoning factor.

In other words, the questions have been chosen to keep vocabulary and other experience elements at the ordinary levels most of us achieve. It is expected, or rather hoped, that you have had as much experience as the next fellow with the cloth from which these problems are cut.

If so, the score will tell you with some accuracy whether you are quite as bright as you always thought you were.

47

Part One:

DIRECTIONS—In each series, certain numbers or letters are left out. Insert the missing numbers or letters. For example: In 2, 4, 6, —, 10, —, 14. you should insert 8 in the first blank and 12 in the second. In A B C — E — G, you should insert D in the first blank and F in the second.

TIME LIMIT: 8 MINUTES

1. 3, 5, 7, 9, 11, 13, 15
2. Z X Y W W U
3. A C E G I K M
4. 100, 200, 400, 800
5. Y E L L O W
6. 9, 7, 11, 9, 13, 11, 15, 13

7. 3, 6, 9, 27, 81, 243
8. 6, 8, 9, 11, 12, 14, 15
9. 1½, 3, 4, 18, 36, 108
10. —, 24, 29, —, 33, 34, 35
11. A B ZYCDX EF
12. 2, 200, 2000, 2000, 200

Part Two:

DIRECTIONS—Fill the blank squares with numbers which will make both the vertical columns and the horizontal rows in each diagram add up to the sum shown at the right of that diagram. Use no number larger than 9, Do not use zero.

TIME LIMIT: 3 MINUTES

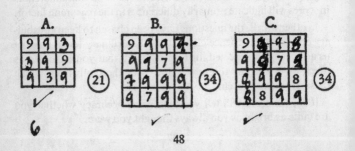

A.

9	9	3
3	9	9
9	3	9

(21)

B.

9	9	9	7
9	9	7	9
7	9	9	9
9	7	9	9

(34)

C.

9	9	9	8
9	9	7	9
9	9	9	8
8	8	9	9

(34)

Part Three:

DIRECTIONS—This is a list of birds, but the letters have been scrambled. Unscramble the letters and in the blank spaces write the words they spell. EGOSO, for example, when unscrambled spells GOOSE.

TIME LIMIT: 2 MINUTES

1. .... Duck .... C K U D ✓
2. .... Gull .... L U L G ✓
3. .... Robin .... N O B R I ✓
4. .... Crow .... W R O C ✓
5. .... Hen .... N H E ✓
6. .... Pigeon .... N O P E I G ✓
7. .... Hawk .... W K H A ✓
8. .... Owl .... L O W ✓
9. .... Parrot .... R O R T A P ✓
10. .... Sparrow .... W A R P S O R ✓
11. .... G E E L A ✗
12. ... Chicken .... K H I E C C N ✓
13. .... Bluebird .... L E U B B R D I ✓
14. .... B B R C L I K D A ✗
15. .... Stork .... K R O T S ✓

6cl ka 13

49

Part Four:
DIRECTIONS—This is a list of animals, but the letters have been scrambled. Unscramble the letters and in the blank spaces write the words they spell. OOMSE, for example, when unscrambled spells MOOSE.

TIME LIMIT: 2 MINUTES

✓ 1...... Cow	W O C
✓ 2...... Tiger	T G E R I
✓ 3...... Horse:	S H E R O
✓ 4... Monkey, ...	Y O M E K N
✗ 5.....................	B A T R I B
✗ 6.....................	R E L Q U I S R
✗ 7.....................	P H E S E
✓ 8...... Cat:	A C T
✓ 9...... Mouse	U E S M O
✓ 10.. Buffalo.	F U L F A B O
✓ 11... Camel.	A M E C L
✗ 12.....................	K K U N S
✗ 13.....................	K Y D E N O
✗ 14.....................	I L G O L A R
✓ 15... Elephant:	H E P L E T A N
✓ 16.... Bear:	B E R A
✓ 17.... Lion	O L I N

Your Score .....
Average Score: 32
SUPERIOR (UPPER TEN PER CENT) 46–62 ✓
GOOD (NEXT TWENTY PER CENT) 38–45
FAIR (NEXT THIRTY PER CENT) 30–37
POOR (LOWEST FORTY PER CENT) 0–29

Section Two:

SKILLS AND TALENTS

8. Have You Musical Talent?

CAN musical talent be measured? Such talent defies analysis or even definition, and among leading psychologists working in this field there is some disagreement as to just what the components of musical talent are.

Take *intelligence*. You might think a fellow would have to be pretty smart to get through his music lessons. And the famous Eastman School of Music, among others, has found it helpful to use intelligence ratings in choosing students. Yet little actual correlation has been found between musical aptitudes and scores on intelligence tests.

What about *acute hearing*, *true pitch*, *tone discrimination* and similar attributes? Surely these would seem to have some bearing on musical ability. Indeed, the Seashore tests and others relying largely on this type of sensory discrimination have in many cases shown significant correlation with apparent musical talent. Yet in as many other studies they have fallen down, yielding no significant indications!

Manual ability, then? Useful perhaps to a violinist, but hardly to a composer. *Spatial relationships*, *mathematical skill* and the like? Useful perhaps to a composer, but hardly to a violinist.

Concerning Your "Ear"

This brings us to *musical memory*—which at least has the merit of wide popular approval as a standard. For the ability to remember melodies, chords and tones is the most commonly accepted measure of musical inclination. It is generally what is meant by the phase "a good ear."

As a matter of fact, tests of musical memory have shown perhaps the highest general correlation with proficiency in music. Yet do they yield any hint concerning the creative power essential to the musical artist? Hardly!

Just the same, examination of the work done in this field and the results achieved does indicate fairly consistent clues to musical talent in certain types of questions. The most frequently encountered characteristic among men recognized as musically talented would seem to be the "good ear for music"—plus the ability to analyze and synthesize what this "good ear" hears! So if you successfully answer all questions in the test which follows, it is pretty safe to assume that you show at least latent musical talent.

Development of Gift

If you make out as well in tests having to do with manual dexterity, the indications are that practice might make you a superior instrumentalist. If you are superior in tests bearing on creativeness, association, and discernment generally, you might be able to develop your musical gift in the direction of composition and orchestration.

This, of course, holds true only if you are not already musically trained. If you are musically experienced, a high score in the test would be more a confirmation of proficiency than an indication of talent.

DIRECTIONS—Needed for this test is a piano and someone to play it, whether yourself or a friend. The test has no time limit. Take all the time you find necessary. Work rapidly rather than slowly, however, as it is the reaction of your ear, rather than your intellect, which is required.

Your Score . . . . .
Average Score: 4
SUPERIOR (UPPER TEN PER CENT) 8–10
GOOD (NEXT TWENTY PER CENT) 6–7
FAIR   (NEXT THIRTY PER CENT) 4–5
POOR (LOWEST FORTY PER CENT) 0–3

1. Underline the title of the melody you consider musically superior.

(a) Yankee Doodle

(b) The Star Spangled Banner

2. Play the phrases below on the piano, or listen to someone else play them. Check the phrase you prefer.

(a)

(b)

3. Play the phrases below on the piano, or listen to someone else play them. Check the phrase you like less.

(a)

(b)

4. Play the chord below on the piano, or listen to someone else play it. Indicate with a check whether you find the chord pleasant or unpleasant.

Pleasant ....

Unpleasant..........

5. Play the chord below on the piano, or listen to someone else play it. Indicate with a check whether you find the chord pleasant or unpleasant.

Pleasant ....

Unpleasant..........

6. Indicate with a check the chord which sounds more agreeable to you.

(a)  (b)

7. Indicate with a check the passage which sounds more agreeable to you.

(a)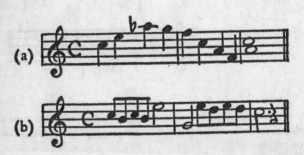

(b)

8. Play the passage below on the piano, or listen while someone else plays it.

With the passage being repeated as many times as you wish, find by experiment any three-note chord which you consider in harmony with it. Write the three notes of this chord............

9. Let a friend twice play the eight notes of the C-scale in ascending order while your back is turned. If the first note is 1, sing or whistle the following:

(a) 2 (b) 3 (c) 7 (d) 5

If your friend, checking immediately after you sound each note, finds that you sing or whistle the tones D—E—B—G, place a check mark at right ....

10. Pay close attention as your friend again plays the C-scale in ascending order. Then let him strike any four notes of the scale in succession while your back is turned. Name the notes, by number, letter or syllable (do, re, mi, etc.).

If he states that you named all four notes correctly, place a check mark at right ....

9. A Head for Figures?

WHILE it does take for granted a certain elementary knowledge of arithmetic, this test is in no sense an achievement test. It is designed to test your flair or bent for mathematical reasoning—for reasoning with mathematical symbols such as numerals—rather than your knowledge of mathematical subjects.

To this end, it contains no questions based on rote calculation or rule. No questions are asked of the "how much is $13 \times 4 - 6 + .5$?" variety, for instance. Nor does the test give you examples in long division, or the finding of a least common denominator. Such questions, encountered often enough in tests for "mathematical ability," are actually memory tests or tests of training. They do not measure your aptitude for reasoning with figures. They show merely whether you remember your multiplication tables or the rules for subtracting fractions, or whether you have had sufficient training to use them swiftly.

Similarly, questions of a geometric nature are not to be found here, although also encountered regularly in so-called "mathematical" tests. These weigh reasoning with shapes and spaces, rather than reasoning with numbers. Psychometric investigation has shown no iron correlation between one aptitude and the other, and indeed seems to indicate that they are more or less independent, perhaps requiring quite different skills.

Low Arithmetical Level

Here you are given the benefit of the doubt. It is assumed you know less arithmetic than a seventh-grade student in elementary school.

The test confines itself to reasoning in, by and with an elementary mathematical alphabet.

Yet if you score high, you would take well to mathematical training even though you may not have any great mathematical knowledge at present. Also, in such types of work where mathematics is an important factor probably you would have a definite edge on others. If you score in the middle group, possibly you would require more effort and more intensive study to be successful in such fields. A low score would indicate in general that it would be difficult for you to make progress in pursuits requiring extensive mathematical reasoning.

DIRECTIONS—Write your answers to each question in the space indicated. Accuracy is more important than speed, but do not linger too long on any one question. You may do rough figuring in the margins or on a separate piece of paper.

TIME LIMIT: 50 MINUTES

1. If 4 apples out of a dozen are bad, how many are good?
Answer (8)

2. In a box of 48 apples, 8 out of each dozen are good. How many in the box are bad?
Answer (16)

3. What number is as much less than 60 as it is more than 50?
Answer (55)

4. A bobby-soxer spent half her money on lunch and half that amount on movies, which left her with 40 cents. How much did she spend on lunch?
Answer (80)

5. How many hours will it take a car to go 400 miles at a speed of 50 miles per hour?
Answer (8)

6. 36 is as much more than 29 as it is less than what number? *Answer* (**43**)

7. Your watch gains 4 minutes in a 24-hour day. If it reads 7 : 30½ at 7 : 30 A.M., how fast will it be at actual noon of the same day?

Answer (   )

8. The sum of A plus B equals 116. A is 3 less than C, but 4 more than B. What number does C equal?

Answer (**63**)

9. If 7 men in 100 are criminals, how many men in 500 are not criminals?

Answer (**465**)

10. Smith, a broker, bought 3 shares at 10 each which he sold at 6 each, and sold at 6 each what he bought at 5 each. If his total profit was 8, how many shares had he bought at 5?

Answer (**23**)

11. How many hours will it take a jet plane to travel 400 miles at a speed of 600 miles per hour?

Answer (**40 mins**)

12. If 6½ yards of upholstery cloth cost 26 dollars, how much will 3½ yards cost?

Answer (**14**)

13. If a grocer has enough eggs to last 300 customers 2 weeks, how long will the eggs last 400 customers?

Answer (**10·5 days**)

14. Suppose A, B and C are numbers. Suppose D is the sum of A, B and C. In that case, would D minus A equal B plus C?
Check one: YES ☑ NO ☐ MAYBE ☐

15. Suppose A and B are numbers. Suppose D is the difference between A and B. In that case, would D plus A equal B, if B is greater than A?
Check one: YES ☑ NO ☑ MAYBE ☐

60

✓ 16. It takes 10 ships 10 days to use 10 tanks of oil. How many days will it take 1 ship to use 1 tank of oil?

Answer (10.)

✗ 17. The winning horse in a race finished at 3 : 01 P.M., 4 lengths in front of the third horse, which finished 2 lengths behind the second horse. The second horse finished 4½ lengths in front of the fourth horse, which ran the race in 61-3/10 seconds. In the last quarter of the race, each horse was traveling one length in one-fifth of a second. At what time did the race begin?

Answer ( )

✗ 18. In this series, what is the next number?

1, 1, 2, 6,

Answer ( )

✗ 19. Supply the missing numbers in this multiplication problem.

$$
\begin{array}{r}
\_\ \_\ \_\ 4 \\
\times\ 6\ \_ \\
\hline
7\ \_\ 5\ 8\ \_ \\
\_\ \_\ \_\ \_\ 4 \\
\hline
\_\ \_\ \_\ \_\ 2\ 6
\end{array}
$$

✓ 20. Suppose the letters in this multiplication problem are numbers. What number does each letter equal?

$$
\begin{array}{r}
2\ F\ 1\ F2 \\
\times\ 2\ E\,3 \\
\hline
6\ 3\ C6 \\
4\,D\ 2\ D4 \\
4\,D\ 8\ B\ C6 \\
\end{array}
$$

212
23

Answer: B= 7 , C= 6 , D= 4 , E= 3 , F= 2

61

21. Suppose the letters in this multiplication problem are numbers, and each blank space represents a missing letter. Supply the missing letters.

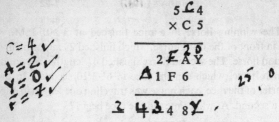

$$5\,\mathcal{L}\,4$$
$$\times\,C\,5$$

C = 4 ✓
A = 2 ✓
Y = 0 ✓
F = 7 ✓

2 E A Y
Δ 1 F 6

22. In a lot of 154 coats, there are 3 less white coats than red coats, but 5 more white coats than green coats. If all the coats are red, white or green, how many red coats are there?

Answer (   )

154

5 4
    5
2 7 2 0
−2 1 7 6
2 4 4 8 0
    1

SUPERIOR (UPPER TEN PER CENT) 17–22

✓GOOD (NEXT TWENTY PER CENT) 14–16

16

FAIR   (NEXT THIRTY PER CENT) 11–13

POOR (LOWEST FORTY PER CENT) 0–10

10. Can You Look Ahead?

THE maze or labyrinth, one of the oldest puzzles devised by humanity, is also one of the most useful as a testing instrument. It is particularly popular in the psychological laboratory, where it is adaptable for the behavior analysis of lesser animals—such as white rats—as well as human beings.

The maze seems to measure anticipation and the ability to foresee, along with speed of learning. If a rat takes fifteen trials to find its way through a maze, it "learns" which are the false turns sooner than a rat which takes, say, thirty trials. However, to the authors' minds such learning is less a matter of reasoning than of conditioned motor reflexes. Every time our rat makes a wrong turn he bumps into a wall—or at least pulls up short and experiences a set of sensations. And so, as the trial proceeds, he comes to avoid the wrong turns reflexively, automatically; not exercising choice in the sense that a reasoning human being does.

For this reason we do not, as many psychologists do, trust the maze to test for learning capacity or reasoning. But if the rat—or the human being—does avoid bumping into walls, then a certain caution is well demonstrated. And if, as in a pencil maze, the walls or obstructions are all visible at the same time, then by selecting a path among them a person does show relative skill in making choices according to what he sees ahead—demonstrates foresight, in other words.

The rat trusts in trial-and-error to get through its maze. But neither the trial-and-error method nor pure chance will enable you to thread these mazes in time, for the choices are too many. You will have to look ahead of your pencil and mentally eliminate undesirable paths.

DIRECTIONS—Starting in the upper left hand corner draw a pencil line through each maze to its exit. Your line is not permitted to cross itself, or any other line. If you do cross a line or go into a blind alley, you may return to the entrance and start over again—or you may pick up where your line turned into the blind alley.

You must attack the mazes in the order given: finish "A" before you start "B," finish "B" before you start "C," and so on.

TIME LIMIT: 5 MINUTES

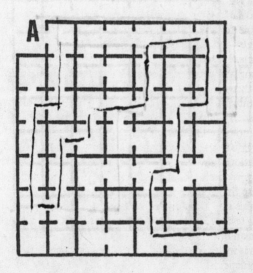

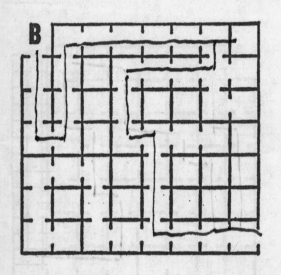

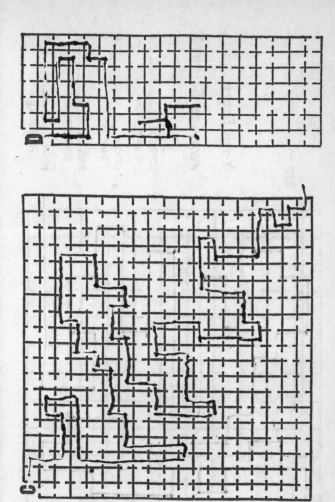

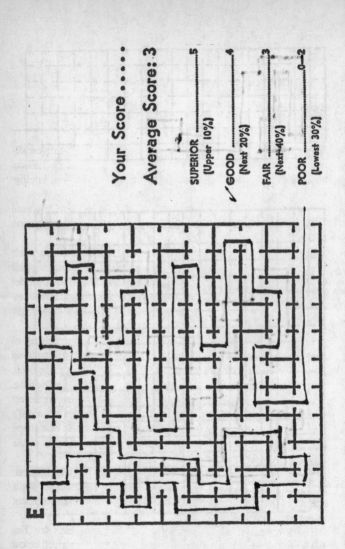

Your Score . . . . .

Average Score: 3

SUPERIOR ———— 5
(Upper 10%)

GOOD ———— 4
(Next 20%)

FAIR ———— 3
(Next 40%)

POOR ———— 0-2
(Lowest 30%)

11. Can You Visualize?

SPATIAL discrimination of one sort or another is universally accepted by psychologists as a vital element in various mechanical and scientific aptitudes—in flair for the graphic arts—in intelligence itself.

Unfortunately, some of the best known and most widely used "spatial" tests fail to bridge the gap between simple perception and actual imagery or reasoning.

These tests require detection of differences, likenesses, parallels in shape and size. They are valuable enough from the standpoint of judging perception—but too often they are presented as guides to intelligence, or as measures of artistic and mechanical aptitudes. Thus used, they are more than inferior; they are downright dangerous!

For when it comes to such aptitudes, the mere perceiving of space characteristics—the "seeing" of them—is not a determining issue. The question is not whether spaces and forms can be seen, but whether they can be used as the raw material of reasoning. Though a blind man cannot "see" his unfinished house, he nevertheless can be told about it and form a picture of it in his mind's eye. And once he does so, he can perhaps figure out the best shape and angle for its roof. Here you have an example of both *spatial imagery* and *spatial reasoning*.

These two are the important spatial factors in the various aptitude complexes, rather than simple sensory perception. As a matter of fact, it can be argued that they are themselves sufficient to demonstrate such perception.

The two are not wholly separable. But the next test (*Are You Inventive?*) stresses the reasoning factor, while the test given below chiefly emphasizes imagery.

Part One:

DIRECTIONS—On the blank line write the number of surfaces each object has. For example:

The object at right has 4 sides, a top and a bottom—or 6 surfaces in all. So you write 6.

A. 6
......

The object at right has 1 top surface, 3 bottom surfaces, 4 outer side surfaces and 2 inner side surfaces—or 10 surfaces in all. So you write 10.

B. 10
......

Study the samples until you are sure you understand the answers you are to make. Then begin the test.

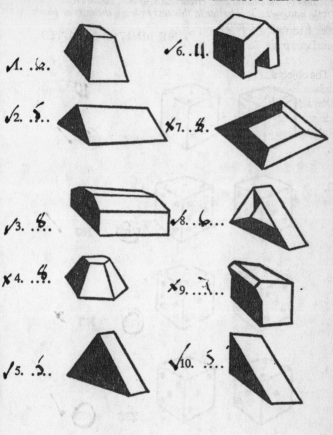

1. ..2.

2. 5..

3. 8...

4. 4...

5. 2...

6. 4..

7. 4..

8. 6...

9. 7...

10. 5...

14

Part Two:

DIRECTIONS—Examine each pair of dice. If, insofar as the dots indicate, the first one of the pair can be turned into the position of the second one, circle YES. If not, circle NO.

Do not guess. It is better in this test to leave the answer blank than to answer wrongly.

TIME LIMIT: 2 MINUTES

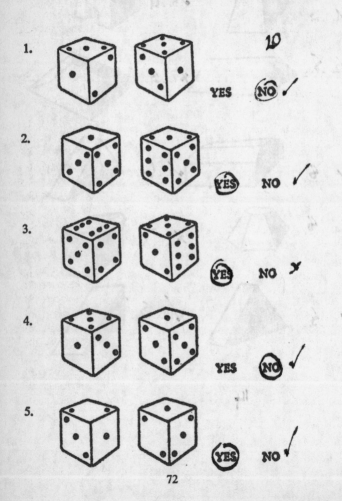

1.   YES   NO

2.   YES   NO

3.   YES   NO

4.   YES   NO

5.   YES   NO

72

Part Three:

DIRECTIONS—In each row, the first drawing represents a solid object. If another drawing in that row shows the same object in a different position, circle the number of that drawing. If no drawing in the row shows the first object, circle NONE.

TIME LIMIT: 1 MINUTE

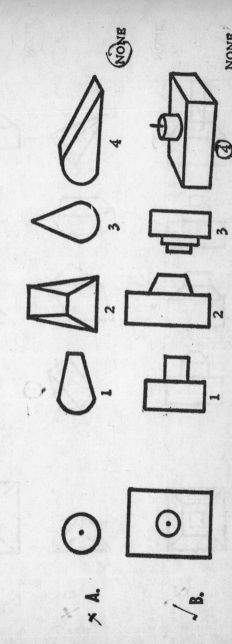

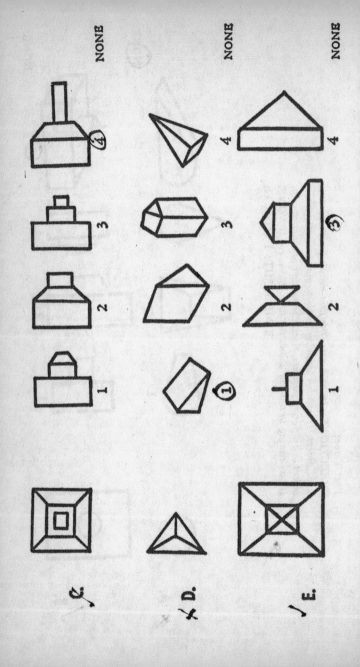

SUPERIOR (UPPER TEN PER CENT)   48–60
GOOD (NEXT TWENTY PER CENT)   41–47
FAIR   (NEXT THIRTY PER CENT)   34–40
POOR (LOWEST FORTY PER CENT)   0–33

12. Are You Inventive?

You come now to the test in *spatial reasoning*, one of the most valuable adaptive tools of the human animal. It is not only a component of general intelligence, but crops up in numerous special aptitudes.

Long aware of its importance, psychologists have developed a number of excellent instruments with which to measure it. These range from the Army Beta subtests to the well known California Test Bureau surveys and the classic Minnesota Form Board. The authors believe that the values of the better tests are to be found combined in the one devised for this book.

Additional Test Factor

It is difficult, maybe not altogether possible, to separate the factors of *visualization* and *reasoning*. Your typical instrument—a cube count, for example—measures both.

But it may be noted that in judging objects whose surfaces are partly hidden (cube tests Beta, MacQuarrie, Thurstone *et al.*), there is no call to combine the visualized spaces into new forms.

Whereas in tests of the Beta geometric and Minnesota types, in which certain forms must be mentally synthesized into still other forms, it is felt by the authors that an additional factor appears. Since it involves ingenuity at combining spaces, this factor is termed *inventiveness*.

Creation and Inventiveness

Creative ability, which has long stumped psychometrists, involves drives, motivations, reaction patterns of a type not claimed to be mirrored in the score of this test. Yet inventiveness has a part in creative ability. And inventiveness can be regarded as a matter of combining existing forms into new ones, of taking elements of old patterns and synthesizing them into new patterns.

Since this spatial reasoning test preserves the *inventiveness* factor, it is separated from the space tests in the previous quiz, *Can You Visualize?* In the authors' view, the score may in a limited way demonstrate your own creative potential. It will more positively demonstrate—and factorial analysis bears this out—your inventiveness with spaces, shapes and forms. Hence the title of the test.

DIRECTIONS—Each of the blank figures on the next page consists of one or more of the numbered shapes in the dark area. In the blank figures write the number of the corresponding shapes.
The shapes may be turned any way in order to make them fit. But you may not use any shape more than once in the same figure.

TIME LIMIT: 4 MINUTES

Your Score . . . . .
Average Score : 54
SUPERIOR (UPPER TEN PER CENT)   67–93
GOOD (NEXT TWENTY PER CENT)   60–66
FAIR   (NEXT THIRTY PER CENT)   52–59
POOR (LOWEST FORTY PER CENT)   0–51

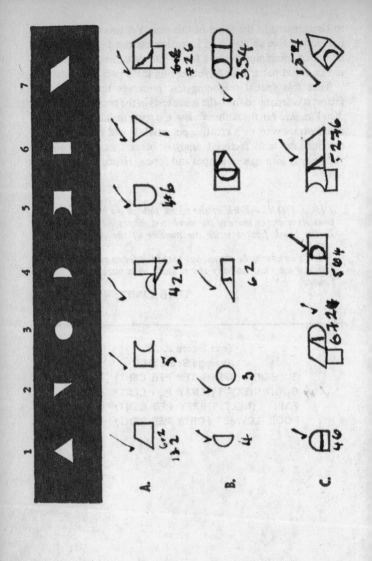

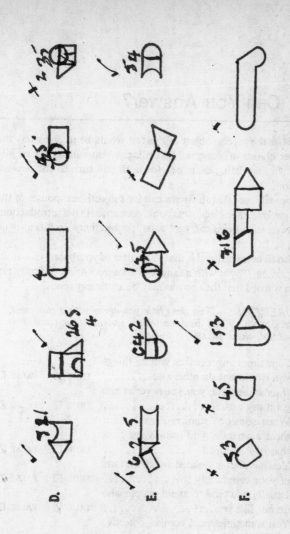

13. Can You Answer?

To NAME the precise object of this test would be to give away the proper choice of answers. Accordingly, you will not learn just what you are being examined for until you turn to the Answer Section.

You will note that the items call for subjective responses of the kind generally avoided in this book. As warned in the Introduction, however, such items carry a "twist"; subjectivity itself is at issue here, so be wary.

Also to be considered is that the matter of vocabulary can affect your rating. Those with a language comprehension difficulty are again warned that their scores may be artificially low.

DIRECTIONS—If on the whole you agree with a statement, check TRUE. *If you disagree with a statement, or consider it doubtful, check* FALSE.

1. Sometimes anger makes you do things you would not do otherwise .... TRUE ☑ FALSE ☐
2. If someone cheats you, you never let him get away with it .... TRUE ☐ FALSE ☑
3. When someone smokes illegally in a theatre or train, you usually see to it that he is stopped .... TRUE ☐ FALSE ☑
4. You have never violated any of the laws of your community .... TRUE ☐ FALSE ☑
5. Usually you tend to avoid people who do not like you.................... TRUE ☑ FALSE ☐
6. You sometimes read comics, detective stories or other "low-brow" writings with enjoyment..................... TRUE ☑ FALSE ☐

7. You believe wholeheartedly in the principle of freedom of speech........ TRUE ☑ FALSE ☐

8. You are not inclined to like people simply because they like you .... TRUE ☑ FALSE ☐

9. When people are less fortunate than yourself, you usually do something to help them .... TRUE ☑ FALSE ☐

10. Being interested in literature, you manage to read most of the good books published each year .... TRUE ☐ FALSE ☑

11. Communist newspapers should be barred from the mails .... TRUE ☐ FALSE ☑

12. Negroes should be allowed to marry white people if they want to .... TRUE ☑ FALSE ☐

13. You are inclined to dislike a person when that person dislikes you ...... TRUE ☑ FALSE ☐

14. All propaganda should be barred from television broadcasts .... TRUE ☑ FALSE ☐

15. The people of every country should be entitled to life, liberty and the pursuit of happiness .... TRUE ☑ FALSE ☐

16. Sometimes you feel a bit "blue" or depressed .... TRUE ☑ FALSE ☐

17. If someone cheats, you never let him get away with it .... TRUE ☐ FALSE ☑

18. You have at least some idea of the meaning of the word PRETORATORY TRUE ☑ FALSE ☐

19. The South American peoples should not be allowed to practice politics dangerous to themselves .... TRUE ☐ FALSE ☑

20. Socialist propaganda should be barred from radio broadcasts .... TRUE ☐ FALSE ☑

21. Negroes are entitled to equality with white people .... TRUE ☑ FALSE ☐

22. On occasion you have seized a choice tid-bit at dinner, although you knew somebody else might have wanted it .. TRUE ☑ FALSE ☐

81

23. At times you pretend to know more than you do .... TRUE ☑ FALSE ☐
24. The German nation, regardless of its record, is entitled to freedom........ TRUE ☑ FALSE ☐
25. When going to the movies with friends, you sometimes want them to attend a picture you prefer rather than one which they prefer .... TRUE ☐ FALSE ☑

Your Score . . . . .
Average Score : 16
SUPERIOR (UPPER TEN PER CENT)   16–25
GOOD (NEXT TWENTY PER CENT)   14–15
FAIR   (NEXT THIRTY PER CENT)   10–13
POOR (LOWEST FORTY PER CENT)   0–9

14. Have You Esthetic Taste?

MANY shrewd tests have been devised by psychometrists to track down one aspect or another of artistic talent—McAdory's scales, for instance, and the Meier-Seashore Art Judgment studies. These classic examples and a variety of more recent ones all follow the same line. They require you to examine a group of carefully graded pictures and select those which you consider superior.

What such tests seek to evaluate is the capacity for artistic judgment—for esthetic taste, in other words. Certainly esthetic taste is the one characteristic most obviously common to artists.

Prejudice Avoided

The test you now are to take uses the classical approach. It permits you to demonstrate your own esthetic judgment within a rudimentary artistic compass. But instead of pictures to compare, you are given schematic drawings. This is done to eliminate considerations of line, tone and color—which involve questions of technique, are grossly subject to individual conditioning, and, in general, lack universality. Also avoided is the halo effect of prejudice for or against the subject matter of actual pictures.

Emphasized instead by this method are unity of form, balance, rhythm and other elements of composition. For humanity after thousands of years is pretty much agreed on what constitutes, good, or at least acceptable, composition. And although composition alone can raise creation to the level of art—as in much so-called "primitive art"—where composition is absent, no art exists.

Talent and Taste

By itself this test can give no hint of whether or not you possess artistic talent. It can tell you, however, whether you do share to some extent a characteristic vital to the artist—and essential to his audience. To appreciate art in any form, to criticize, understand or profoundly enjoy it, you must possess taste—a flair for the beautiful and the fitting.

Incidentally, it does not appear that such taste is inborn. Psychological research inclines toward the view that sound esthetic judgment is largely a matter of cultivation and experience.

Part One:
DIRECTIONS—Check the sketch in each row which best illustrates the word at the left of that row.

NO TIME LIMIT

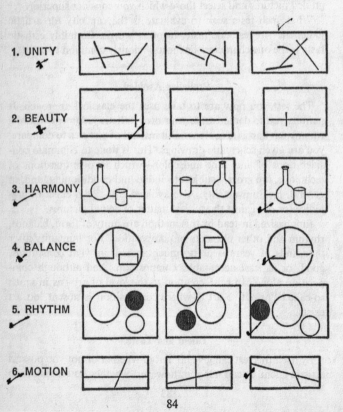

1. UNITY

2. BEAUTY

3. HARMONY

4. BALANCE

5. RHYTHM

6. MOTION

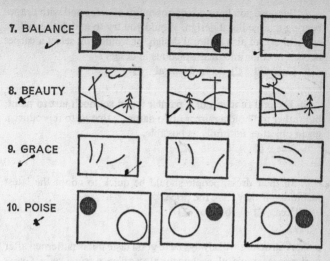

7. BALANCE

8. BEAUTY

9. GRACE

10. POISE

Part Two:

DIRECTIONS—Check the phrase which on the whole is the best answer to the question, or which best completes the statement.

NO TIME LIMIT

1. Joe Doe is 5 feet 4 inches tall and weighs 200 pounds, which makes him a pretty plump person by any standard. Which pattern do you recommend for his suit?

   a. Large over-all plaid □
   b. Faint pin-stripe □
   c. Strong, well-spaced vertical stripes ☑

2. Select the best fit for the same Mr. Doe's suits.

   a. Loose, easy drape □
   b. Neither loose nor form-fitting ☑
   c. Form-fitting □

3. Can it be in good taste to place a *modern* chair and sofa in a room which contains "period" furniture?

   a. Yes □   b. No ☑

85

4. Suppose you have a long room full of color and with drapes bearing a large floral design. Would you try to match this with a colorful carpet also of floral design, or would you select a carpet neutral in color and inconspicuous in design?

    a. Colorful ☐   b. Neutral ☑

5. The real function of a painter is not so much just to paint, but rather to "hold a mirror up to nature"; that is, to reproduce a given object as faithfully as possible.

    a. Yes ☐   b. No ☑

6. In their dress, people should be quick to adopt the latest fashions—if they have the price.

    a. Yes ☐   b. No ☑

7. A structure will always be in good taste if it is patterned after a classic example of architectural excellence, such as a Greek temple or a Gothic church.

    a. Yes ☐   b. No. ☑

8. Large furniture in a small room will make the room appear larger.

    a. Yes ☐
    b. No ☑
    c. Sometimes ☐

9. Small women look better in waist-length jackets than do tall women.

    a. Yes ☐
    b. No ☑
    c. Yes, if the jacket is of chinchilla ☐

10. Pictures of different sizes and shapes generally look better when hung—

    a. With the *tops* of the frames on one level ☑
    b. With the *bottoms* of the frames on one level ☐

15. Are You Artistic?

PREFERENCE tests like those in the preceding quiz (*Have You Esthetic Taste?*) are often represented as measuring artistic talent. We have seen that they do no such thing. Esthetic appreciation, while requisite to the artist, is only part of his special bent—and a non-creative part.

What's more, many keen psychologists are suspicious of the preference method even as a yard-stick of taste. True, preference scale items are labeled "good" or "bad" according to the judgment of supposedly competent art authorities. True, such judgment supposedly derives from centuries of human experience. Just the same, it can be argued that the preference method shows not independent artistic taste at all—but merely how well a person conforms to accepted art standards.

Is there any measurable aptitude, then, which might give some index to artistic talent?

Well, obviously the artist can express himself only if he has a certain amount of technique. Perhaps it is possible to predict whether a person can acquire sufficient technique to draw, paint or otherwise perform in pictorial mediums. Such techniques can be learned. But the man with artistic talent learns them more quickly, more easily and often with less teaching. Indeed, this technical facility more often than not is the very mark which sets him apart from other people.

Trend in Measurement

In modern art-talent tests, therefore, the trend is to rely less on preference scales and more on measures of technical capacity. The test which follows is typical.

Its aim is to establish whether you can develop the technical mastery essential in pictorial art. By this is meant not motor or manual proficiency, for investigation has shown these to have little to do with artistic talent. The issue, rather, is your capacity to retain, analyze and reproduce images—a special form of spatial adjustment which appears to lie at the bottom of pictorial technique.

DIRECTIONS—Examine each framed drawing separately, and check as indicated by the question or statement within the frame.

Work slowly and carefully. Remember that the drawing in any one frame is distinct from every other, and has its own particular set of characteristics.

NO TIME LIMIT

1. This is a group of buildings viewed from an airplane. Could the buildings be parallel? YES.✓.. NO..........

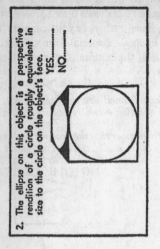

2. The ellipse on this object is a perspective rendition of a circle roughly equivalent in size to the circle on the object's face.
   YES..........
   NO..........

3. The topmost glass is in accurate perspective. Are the other two glasses in roughly accurate perspective? YES.......... NO.✓..

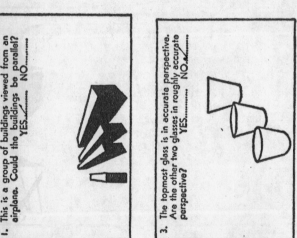

4. (a) This figure is drawn in roughly accurate perspective? YES.......... NO.✓..
   (b) The surfaces visible could be exterior surfaces. YES.✓.. NO..........
   (c) The surfaces visible could be interior surfaces. YES.......... NO.✓..

6. Which edge, if altered, would put this drawing into perspective?

8. Imagine that the light is directly over this folded tape. Which surfaces, other than ground surfaces, should be shadowed?

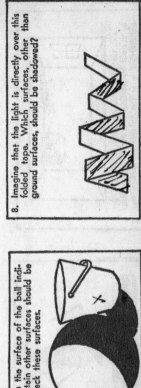

5. Check the fewest number of edges which, if altered, would put this drawing into consistent perspective.

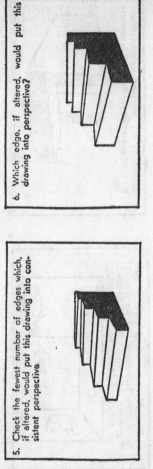

7. The shadow on the surface of the ball indicates that certain other surfaces should be shadowed. Check these surfaces.

9. Judging by the surfaces already shadowed, which other surfaces of this folded strip should be shadowed?

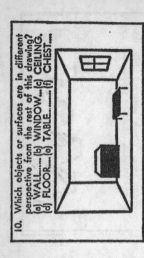

10. Which objects or surfaces are in different perspective from the rest of this drawing?
(a) WALL...... (b) WINDOW.... (c) CEILING.
(d) FLOOR.... (e) TABLE..... (f) CHEST....

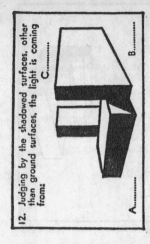

11. Which objects or surfaces are in different perspective from the rest of the drawing?
(a) WALL....... (b) WINDOW....(c) CEILING.
(d) FLOOR.....(e) COUCH...... (f) CHEST....

12. Judging by the shadowed surfaces, other than ground surfaces, the light is coming from:

A.............

C............

B.............

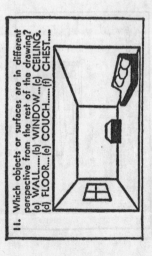

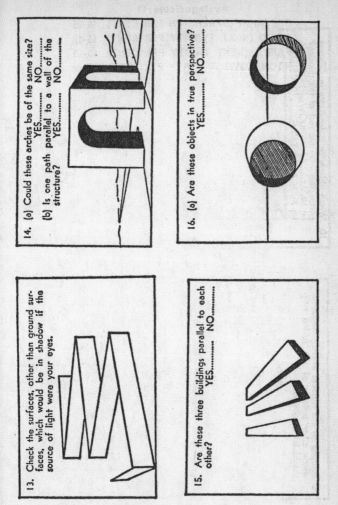

13. Check the surfaces, other than ground surfaces, which would be in shadow if the source of light were your eyes.

14. (a) Could these arches be of the same size? YES......... NO.........
(b) Is one path parallel to a wall of the structure? YES......... NO.........

15. Are these three buildings parallel to each other? YES......... NO.........

16. (a) Are these objects in true perspective? YES......... NO.........

93

Average Score : 13

SUPERIOR (UPPER TEN PER CENT) 19–25
GOOD (NEXT TWENTY PER CENT) 16–18
FAIR   (NEXT THIRTY PER CENT) 13–15
POOR (LOWEST FORTY PER CENT)   0–12

16. What's Your Art S—R?

THERE remains to be tested another side of the artistic personality, having to do with imagination, suggestibility and sensitivity to stimuli. These qualities are among the identifying marks of the creative artist. The suggestible and sensitive, while not always reacting more powerfully to stimuli than the phlegmatic, do react more quickly—and to lesser stimuli. The result is that your sensitive person is more often the one stimulated into the reaction-syndromes known as expression.

Imagination an Essential

As for imagination, it is the first and most vital weapon in the creative arsenal. Pictures, like machines, start as visions. Only after initial conception in the brain can they be rendered into substance by the hands and other parts of the body.

We have noted that esthetic taste, one characteristic of the artist, is essentially a passive quality—a quality of appreciation rather than creation. Similarly, analytical understanding of space, line and shadow, while important to pictorial expression, cannot itself bestow creativeness. It is imagination which appears to be at the bottom of the creative process. And the more facile, more easily evoked reactions of the sensitive, suggestible person make a given stimulus more likely to trigger his imagination into motion. Further, sensitivity in human beings is associated not only with a more easily stirred imagination, but frequently with a stronger and more vivid one.

95

The test ladder which follows provides certain sets of stimuli. Your reactions to these complete a stimulus-response (S—R) cycle, yielding an index of the extent to which they pique your imagination. Hence your score will tell you how sensitive you are in comparison with other people, judged on the basis of your imaginative responses.

DIRECTIONS—Every drawing on the opposite page suggests 1 or more words listed below. Your job is to find the suggested words and write their numbers under each drawing. You may use any listed word even remotely suggested by the drawing.

Choose from 1 to 3 words for each drawing. Even when 1 word seems adequate, use up to 3 words if you consider them at all appropriate.

And remember, you may use a listed word for more than 1 drawing.

NO TIME LIMIT

1. EVIL	21. HOT	41. NERVOUS
2. DANCE	22. BITTER	42. CALM
3. SAHARA	23. DOUBT	43. JOY
4. PUMPKIN	24. RHYTHM	44. ELASTIC
5. TRAVEL	25. REST	45. ORNAMENT
6. PLAY	26. SLEEP	46. ECSTASY
7. SALTY	27. PAIN	47. GAME
8. CONFUSION	28. ANGER	48. ANIMAL
9. FLIGHT	29. POWER	49. SPACE
10. BRIGHT	30. HORN	50. FEAR
11. CHEMISTRY	31. ATOMIC	51. SHARP
12. PHYSICS	32. BACTERIA	52. NEATNESS
13. FOOD	33. ROBOT	53. PRIMNESS
14. WIND	34. GRACEFUL	54. WORSHIP
15. GEOMETRY	35. PEACE	55. SWEET
16. WORRY	36. NOISY	56. SOUR
17. THIRST	37. SEX	57. CRUEL
18. STORM	38. MASK	58. HORROR
19. ELECTRIC	39. BOSOM	59. PIE
20. RADIO	40. LIFE	60. SEA

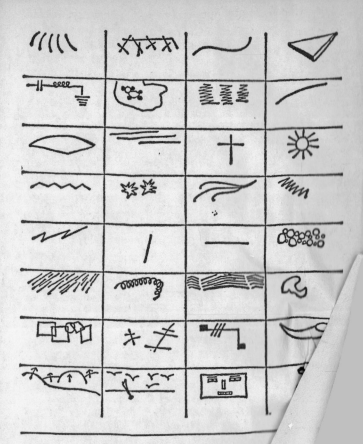

Your Score . . . . .

Average Score : 50

SUPERIOR (UPPER TEN PER CE

GOOD (NEXT TWENTY PER C

FAIR (NEXT THIRTY PER

POOR (LOWEST FORTY P

Section Three:

PERSONALITY

17. Can You Succeed?

Not much introduction is needed here. Enough to say that there is
one human quality important beyond all others to success in this
life. Without specifying what the precious quality is—which is
done in the Answer Section rather than here—this tricky test lets
you demonstrate whether or not you possess it. Be careful!

> *DIRECTIONS—With a pencil in your hand, study the diagram
> on the next page as long as you like. Then close your eyes, lift the
> pencil over your head to the full height of your arm, and see how
> many bull's-eyes you can score with the pencil-point. You have 5
> tries in all. Remember, the only hits which count are those
> landing in the white area dead-center of each target.*
>
> NO TIME LIMIT

First try: HIT.............. MISS..................
Second try: HIT.............. MISS................
Third try: HIT.............. MISS..................
Fourth try: HIT.............. MISS.................
Fifth try: HIT.............. MISS..................

18. Are You a good Lover?

THE next test examines the attitudes you bring to love, and also your skill in implementing these attitudes. For the lover must strike a nice balance between his natural emotions and impulses on the one hand, and on the other the gentle artifices sometimes required to put across his feelings. If such artifice is generous and employed for giving rather than taking, it has its place. If employed for self-aggrandizement, for tickling one's own ego, it is dangerous. In any event, if too much relied on, artifice leads to a forced relationship.

Thus it sometimes comes off quite well to pattern your love-making after the smooth ways of glamor folk you see on the screen. But if you are not a glamor boy or girl yourself, on more intimate acquaintance your sweetie-pie will pierce the false front, feel disappointment and chagrin, perhaps leave you. The best rule to follow is: Be yourself.

Yet it helps also to keep in the position of the giver, without being cunning or calculating about it. The cynic may scoff at poets who sing of love as an unselfish emotion, but wise is the lover who takes his cue from such sentiments. For true love—and successful love—is a matter of give and take, with the emphasis chiefly on the "give."

To be sure, a lover must bear in mind that his (or her) beloved may also wish to be a bestower rather than a taker. The rule here is to do what makes your beloved happy. By letting your emotions control you fully at such times you will take warmly and deeply of all that love offers—which itself can be a high form of giving.

DIRECTIONS—Check YES if on the whole you agree with a statement. Check NO if you are inclined to disagree. Try to answer every question. Work as slowly as you like.

NO TIME LIMIT

✓ 1. A person should be even more polite to a loved one than to strangers.

YES........ NO..✓.....

✓ 2. On the whole, the traditional, time-tested roles should be maintained between lovers—that is, male dominant, female submissive.

YES........ NO..✓.....

✓ 3. While with his (or her) sweetheart, a person sees a particularly gorgeous member of the opposite sex. Should this person stifle any impulse to express admiration for the attractive stranger?

YES........ NO..✓.....

✓ 4. A person's love-making routine should be down pat enough so that he (or she) will not stumble, fumble or appear silly.

YES........ NO..✓.....

5. If really in love, a person should: (*Check one*)
(a) Take the trouble to memorize eloquent love passages from literature, so that these can be repeated to his (or her) beloved
....
(b) Choose passages from current magazine stories instead, as these are more up-to-date and less hackneyed..............
(c) Try to find romantic phrases in the love letters of famous people encountered in biographies, libraries, etc. ....
✓(d) Just don't bother to look for nicely turned love phrases which might help ✗....................................

✓ 6. A person should be even more considerate of a loved one than of strangers.

YES...✓.... NO........

104

✓ 7. A lover—as the advertisements recommend—should give particular attention to personal cleanliness, sweet breath and the like before going on a date.

YES.✓..... NO........

✓ 8. A person's love-making should be fairly predictable so as not to startle his (or her) loved one.

YES........ NO.✓.....

✓ 9. A couple in love should make each other feel that nothing is as important as the love between them by confining most of their conversation to amorous and personal matters.

YES........ NO.✓.....

✓ 10. It is perfectly moral for a girl to make overtures to a man who attracts her, or whom she thinks she loves.

YES..✓.... NO........

✓ 11. In no more than 25 words, write how you would ask someone you love for a kiss..................

.............*Can I have a kiss*..................

....

....

✓ 12. If a person can manage self-control and rigid mastery of his behavior in the presence of the opposite sex, he (or she) has an advantage on less careful persons when it comes to making love.

YES........ NO.✓.....

13. At a party, a girl meets a man who strongly attracts her. A week later she telephones him, and either asks him for a date or strongly hints that he ask her for one.

✗ (a) He might consider her action improper.

YES........ NO.✓.....

✓ (b) You consider her action improper.

YES........ NO.✓.....

(c) Her action might not be good tactics, for he might think her too bold. Better if she didn't risk losing his good opinion.

YES........ NO........

14. Some girls like the lobe of an ear kissed; others prefer holding hands. Should a person try to furnish the kind of loving his (or her) opposite number prefers?

YES........ NO........

15. One's love-making technique should not be too predictable, even if this sometimes results in startling one's sweetheart.

YES........ NO........

16. The person who loves another should come out with it and frankly say so, rather than make his love known by means of innuendos, sighs, glances, gifts and the like.

YES........ NO........

17. When true love is shared by a couple it automatically endures, needing neither stimulation nor attention to keep it alive.

YES........ NO........

18. To provoke genuine love it is best, perhaps, that a person be artless and even innocent. But in order to sustain such love over the course of years, should that person abandon artlessness and deliberately cultivate craft in the techniques of love?

YES........ NO........

19. Suppose a person has not much money to spend on gifts to a loved one. In that case, he or she should: (*Check one*)
   (a) Buy no gifts at all....................................
   (b) Buy "practical" gifts only, such as shoes or clothing......
   (c) Buy flowers or baubles once in a while................

20. The romantic "love" so widely sung by poets is a kind of love all right for dreamers and impractical people, but it is quite unsuitable for ordinary, hard-working men and women.

YES........ NO........

106

Your Score . . . . .
Average Score : 12
20 ✓ SUPERIOR (UPPER TEN PER CENT)   17–22
GOOD (NEXT TWENTY PER CENT)   14–16
FAIR   (NEXT THIRTY PER CENT)   11–13
POOR (LOWEST FORTY PER CENT)   0–10

19. Do People Like You?

WIDELY used in schools and industrial firms are certain commercially available measuring instruments which try to gauge social adjustment through questions of this nature:

Do some people make such foolish remarks that you should contradict them?

Are the beliefs of certain people so stupid that you should condemn those beliefs?

Do you intently dislike certain people because they are so unreasonable?

In each case the answer is supposed to be *No*. If you answer *Yes*, you are assumed to lack social skill or social standards, or to show "withdrawal" tendencies—which in turn is taken to mean that you are unpopular or otherwise maladjusted socially.

By this line of reasoning a social premium is placed on unctuousness and lack of moral fibre. All of which is nonsense—from the scientific standpoint. On the question of popularity, any extensive sampling will show that your spineless fellow—while rarely the most disliked—is quite as rarely the most liked.

If a man states to your face that Hitler was a great guy—are you supposed to keep silent? If the foreman at your plant unreasonably exploits you, are you supposed not to condemn him, not to dislike him? Even if such a course did win popularity, it would be popularity with whom? With the very persons you care least about, whose affections are least flattering! Almost every one of us, openly or secretly, hungers for affection and approval. In the scientific view this is a valuable psychological phenomenon, a device whereby the ego is nourished and renewed. But being liked by the "wrong" persons does not feed the healthy ego. If a man is known to others by the company he keeps, so also is he known to himself.

Social Skills are Important

Denial of your moral principles or personality cannot make people cherish you. At best it can induce them to tolerate you—for the reason that you do not register on them much one way or the other.

The social skills may help you to be liked, but they do not consist of negation—rather they are matters of discretion, tact and approach. Who has the greater social skill—he who ducks an unpopular issue, or he who can argue it without arousing hostility? Without being artful or dishonest, we can all act in a way that implies recognition of other people's virtues. If we forego the pleasure of puffing our own self-esteem, if we make others feel comfortable and relaxed—and appreciated—we can generally get them to like us.

The questions listed will give an indication of whether you have the coveted knack of evoking fondness and liking.

DIRECTIONS—Check YES if on the whole you can agree with a statement. Check NO if you are inclined to disagree. Try to answer every question. Work as slowly as you like.

NO TIME LIMIT

In order to be liked:

1. A person should keep in mind that almost every minute of the day he is under the scrutiny of those with whom he comes in contact.

YES........ NO.........

2. A person should be independent enough to talk freely to friends about a pet interest or hobby whether or not they share his enthusiasm.

YES......... NO........

3. It is wisest to preserve dignity even when strongly tempted to do otherwise.

YES......... NO........

✓ 4. When a person is smart enough to catch flaws in the casual conversation of others, he should make it his business to try and straighten them out.

YES........ NO.✓......

✓ 5. When meeting strangers, one should try to be charming and witty enough to impress them.

YES........ NO.✓......

✓ 6. When being introduced to another whose name he does not catch, a person should ask that the name be repeated.

YES..✓..... NO........

✓ 7. A person should make sure that he is respected by never permitting himself to become the butt of a joke.

YES........ NO..✓......

✓ 8. A person should be wary lest others play tricks on him so that he is laughed at.

YES........ NO..✓......

✓ 9. When talking with someone whose conversation is witty and sparkling, a person should make an honest attempt at clever answers and *repartee*.

YES........ NO.✓......

✓ 10. A person should always be careful to reflect the mood of the company he is in.

YES..✓..... NO........

✓ 11. A person should help his friends because a time may come when he badly needs help from them.

YES..✓..... NO........

✓ 12. It doesn't pay to do too many favors, because after all, how many people really appreciate them?

YES........ NO.✓......

13. It is better for a person to have others depend on him than for him to depend on others.

YES........ NO.✓......

14. A real friend makes an effort to help those who are objects of his friendship.

YES..✓.... NO........

15. A person should keep putting his best foot forward to make sure he is really approved of and appreciated.

YES........ NO.✓......

16. At a party, a person who has previously heard a joke should stop another who wants to tell it.

YES........ NO✓......

17. At a party, a person who has previously heard a joke should be polite enough to laugh heartily when another tells it.

YES........ NO✓......

18. When a person is invited to a friend's home but prefers to go to the movies, he should say that he had a headache or give some other mild excuse, rather than risk hurting the friend's feelings by telling the truth.

YES........ NO.✓......

19. A real friend insists that those close to him do the things that are best for them even when they don't want to.

YES........ NO.✓......

20. A person should not boldly and forcefully defend his beliefs every time someone happens to express a contrary opinion.

YES....✓... NO..✗....

SUPERIOR (UPPER TEN PER CENT) 85–100
GOOD (NEXT TWENTY PER CENT) 75–80
FAIR   (NEXT THIRTY PER CENT) 65–70
POOR (LOWEST FORTY PER CENT) 0–60

20. Are You Really Happy?

BEFORE psychological science attained its present stature, it might have seemed queer to ask whether an apparently happy person were *really* happy. But today it is known that we may conceal even from ourselves the primal fears, anxieties and insecurities which so often gnaw people from within. Often the man who considers himself fortunate nevertheless cannot help feeling pangs and dissatisfactions which can only be described as unhappiness, while many a person who considers himself unhappy is actually more happy than most.

Human Happiness Is Complex

Happiness to a certain extent can be regarded as lack of desire; or more properly, as lack of the kind of desire which cannot be fulfilled. A pig, for instance, easily attains happiness because his chief desire is to swill, and usually he can do so.

In human beings the process is more difficult because human desires are both more numerous and more complex than those of the pig—and more often impossible to satisfy. Further, we have all observed that frequently people are happier while working toward a coveted goal than they are once the goal is achieved. So lack of unfulfilled, or unfulfillable, desire—the state we call contentment—is not the whole story.

Apparently a certain amount of nascent desire, of expectation, plays its part in the happiness pattern. This is in line with the psychological concept of the human being as a stimulus-response machine. When exposed to the stimulus, say, of a porterhouse steak, a hungry man responds with eager eye and watering mouth. He has one desire at the moment, and is happy in the expectation of its easy satisfaction. If inhibited by anxiety about digestion, he would not be so happy. But not being thus repressed, he advances an ardent fork, pokes a morsel into his mouth, and experiences pleasure—technically, the satisfying of a want, the sensation of appropriate response to a given stimulus. And when the steak is devoured, having no further desire, he is momentarily content.

But contentment vanishes swiftly, and with it some portion of happiness. For it is a psychological axiom that every response is itself a stimulus, and calls for a new response. The man full of steak now craves bicarbonate of soda!

Happiness a Comparative State

The chain of stimulus-response, conditioned by circumstances, stretches from cradle to the grave, making the normal person a creature of constant dissatisfactions. Therefore when we speak of happiness, we speak of *relative* happiness. Indeed, the too complete absence of desire and irritation (as in sleep) is akin to death.

Here a clue is sought not only to whether your desires are withheld from fulfillment by psychological barriers, but also to whether you have eligible desires at all—desires which lend themselves to easy fulfillment, and so are the stuff of happiness. A high score would suggest that you are really happy in comparison with most others, whether you know it or not.

DIRECTIONS—Check YES if on the whole you agree with a statement. Check NO if you are inclined to disagree. Try to answer every question. Work as slowly as you like.

NO TIME LIMIT

✓1. On the whole, crowds are depressing and should be avoided on that account.

YES........ NO. ✓......

✓2. People who are meticulous, painstaking and neat are usually preferable to less orderly people.

YES........ NO..✓.......

114

✓3. A person should always count on the fact that his schemes are likely to fail.

YES........ NO..✓.....

✗4. A person should always count on the fact that his schemes will succeed.

YES...✓.... NO........

✓5. Despite the universal acceptance of sleeping in darkness, it is really more pleasant to sleep in a place where there is a little light.

YES........ NO.✓......

✓6. It's usually nicer to lie awake in bed in the morning rather than get up soon after awakening.

YES........ NO.✓......

/7. A person should often indulge in idle day-dreams in which he imagines himself achieving marvelous deeds.

YES...✗.... NO..✓.....

✓8. A person is the master of his fate, and the sole factor in determining his own success or failure.

YES........ NO..✓.....

✗9. It's all right for a person to spend so much time at a hobby that at times it interferes with his social life or business.

YES........ NO.✓......

✓10. Women generally are difficult to be at ease with.

YES........ NO.✓......

✓11. On the whole, women are considerably superior to men.

YES........ NO.✓......

✓12. People in most fields of work get paid too much.

YES........ NO.✓.....

115

13. Are you shrewd enough to notice often that people are apparently talking about you, perhaps smiling secretly at the things you do?

YES........ NO........

14. Women in general are more unfair and scheming than men.

YES........ NO........

15. To avoid the trouble which mars happiness, a person should only act after he has so thoroughly weighed pros and cons that there is no doubt in his mind about which course to take.

YES........ NO........

16. Are you sensitive enough to nearly always know when you are criticized more than you deserve?

YES........ NO........

17. (a) People require a certain amount of money to be happy.

YES........ NO........

(b) Unhealthy people are rarely happy.

YES........ NO........

(c) Generally speaking, people should not marry persons they do not love.

YES........ NO........

18. (a) Do you believe in God?

YES........ NO........

(b) Do you believe in Communism or Socialism?

YES........ NO........

(c) Do you believe in atheism?

YES........ NO........

(d) Have you faith that the West will triumph over Russia?

YES........ NO........

19. Do you believe in any philosophy—religion—any system of human thought or organization?

YES........ NO........

✓ 20. Assume there are people you deeply trust and rely on. In that case:

(a) You are foolish, because in the end practically every person lets others down.

TRUE........ FALSE..✓.....

(b) You are not foolish, because your feelings tell you that you can trust these people, and you want to do so.

TRUE..✓.... FALSE........

(c) You are not foolish, because you know that you can place full reliance and trust in most people you run across.

TRUE........ FALSE..✓.....

Your Score .....
Average Score : 14

✓EXCELLENT   (UPPER TEN PER CENT)   17–22
GOOD   (NEXT TWENTY-FIVE PER CENT)   15–16
FAIR   (NEXT THIRTY-FIVE PER CENT)   12–14
INFERIOR   (LOW THIRTY PER CENT)   0–11

21. Can You Take It?

THE big question to be decided now is whether unexpected situations and the necessity for split-second decisions throw you off center. Does the rush act put your head in a whirl? Or are you one of those fortunate individuals whose brains can rise to the occasion?

The amusing quiz given below falls into the "complicated directions" class included in some of the better known mental test batteries. Many top psychologists believe that the ability to follow complex directions is itself an index of mental capacity—or more specifically, of attention span and concentration. You can judge your score from that standpoint, if you wish.

But this ability has been found to show less correlation with *I. Q.* than certain others, and so is omitted from the general intelligence rating (*page 8*). It is weighed here, under special time conditions, primarily to discover if you keep your mental equanimity and poise under stress. If so, like the "money player" in sports, you can be at your best when the chips are down.

A good score would strongly hint that your mind can take it when it comes to complications under time pressure. Of the sample (adult) group tested, the highest 10 per cent scored 19 or higher, while the next 20 per cent made from 14 to 15 points. The next 30 per cent scored 12 to 13 right. Count your correct answers and see into which group you fit. Less than 12 correct shows that you may tend to become unduly confused in unfamiliar situations requiring rapid brainwork.

DIRECTIONS—Simply follow as best you can the instructions in the paragraph below.

TIME LIMIT: 5 MINUTES

If the letter Z appears anywhere before this comma, cross it out —otherwise cross it out in this word: ZOO. Now unless the word

118

word appears in sword draw a wavy line here.........., otherwise draw a cross; and by the way, if A is number 1 in the alphabet, what does JM total? ....If dogs chase cats and cats chase mice tell what single-figure odd number becomes even when viewed upside-down.........., otherwise draw a cross........ Don't write DISCURSIVE here..............if the word does not contain all of the vowels, but instead write the first four vowels in the alphabet. Now go back to the first sentence and circle the word ZOO unless a circle cannot represent any letter of the alphabet. So much for the alphabet, except that if C is not the third letter don't draw a square in this space..........but do draw a cow's ear at the bottom of the page, unless D is not the second letter, in which case draw a human ear, unless you can't draw a human ear. If EAR rhymes with HAIR draw an ear anyway. Can you count from 10 down to 5? Do this backwards, writing the numbers on this line...................... Now if a BAT can be a bird or not an animal, don't draw a ball at the left of this line, but write there the letters which appear least often in ABRACA-DABRA. Punctuate this sentence to make sense: THAT THAT IS IS. Then if the wrong answer to "What is the largest state?" is "Texas," write CALIFORNIA here............otherwise in the same space don't write ZOWIE unless deer hear. Draw a line over the second word in this sentence and under the second word in the next sentence. Write three words ending in X at the top o this page. Write XYZ at the left of the page if a circle is not a square: wait! Write it at the right of the page instead unless a circle is sometimes bigger than a square. Next, give the wrong answer to the negative of this question: HOW OLD ARE YOU? ....Now if you've had enough write UNCLE at the end of this sentence, otherwise write UNCLE.

Your Score . . . . .
Average Score: 13

119

22. How's Your Judgment?

SHREWD and prudent judgment is encountered in only a minor percentage of human beings, and like most rare possessions is especially prized by those who do not have it. Yet judgment is less a natural gift than a cultivated habit of mind. It can be acquired at least in some degree by all—provided they have the capacity to observe and reason, and will take the trouble to do so.

What most frequently interferes with accurate judgment is sheer laziness, with prejudice not far behind. Lazy, slovenly thought habits give rise to the universal human disease of jumping to conclusions; a disease whose symptom is blithe disregard for available facts. As for prejudice, it makes a person unable to respond to facts at all, so that his decisions are those of a man chloroformed or sleep-walking.

Careful thinking, plus open-mindedness rather than prejudice, are the keys to good judgment. Caution in coming to any conclusion, if cultivated to the point of habit, will cause the individual to rely on these qualities in small as well as large matters, with resultant help in his daily judgments.

There is plenty of time in this test to observe and weigh the information given, to take note of apparently small but perhaps quite important points. Note that you are penalized *two* points rather than one for each wrong answer, so don't guess—just use your judgment!

DIRECTIONS—Check the correct answer to each question listed. Do not check any incorrect answers.

NO TIME LIMIT

1. If goods and services produced this year in the United States have a value of 500 billion dollars—and assuming that thermonuclear bombs or the like do not destroy mankind—then goods

and services produced a thousand years from now will have what annual value?

A ....More than 1600 billion.

B ....More than 1500 billion.

C ....Less than 1500 billion.

D ....Probably 1900 billion.

(If you cannot answer, check here. ✗......)

2. Considering recent progress in atomic research, how many years will it be before scientists are able to split the gold atom?

A ....Ten years.

B ....Twenty years.

C ....About twenty years.

D ....More than twenty years.

E ....About fifty years.

F ....A hundred years.

G ....Never.

(If you cannot answer, check here. ✗......)

3. A man adds a long column of figures five times and gets the following sums: (a) 32,501 (b) 32,503 (c) 32,501 (d) 31,405 (e) 32,503 Which sum is most likely to be correct?

A An average of the five sums.

B ..✗....32,501.

C ....32,503.

D ....32,501 or 32,503.

(If you cannot answer, check here........)

4. Total production of fountain pens in the United States during a recent year was 14,000,000. The pens varied in length from 3 to 6 inches, with more than 80 per cent averaging 5 inches. If all the pens were laid end to end, how far would they reach?

A ....About a thousand miles.

B ....About half across the Pacific.

C ....Between 1,000 and 1,104 miles.

D ....Between 1,000 and 1,500 miles.

(If you cannot answer, check here........)

5. What is the underlying flaw in the logic of this statement?

There are 365 days in a year. Mr. Smith sleeps 8 hours a day, or about 122 days, leaving 243 days. Mr. Smith spends another hour each day traveling to and from work, and 7 hours a day on reading, recreation and the like. This accounts for another 122 days leaving 121 days. Subtracting 52 Sundays leaves 69 days. But an hour and 20 minutes each day for meals adds up to 20 days, leaving 49 days. Also, Mr. Smith takes a half-day off on Saturdays which accounts for another 26 days, leaving 9 days. But Mr· Smith's company is closed on the 9 legal holidays in a year· Therefore Mr. Smith is left with no time to work!

A ......The statement mentions that Mr. Smith travels "to and from work." Therefore, he *does* work—which contradicts the whole statement!

B ......The statement counts certain hours more than once. For instance, the year's sleeping hours (amounting to 122 days) are deducted. But 52 Sundays are also deducted, without making allowance for the sleeping hours already withdrawn from those Sundays.

C ......The statement is incorrect because no working person spends 7 hours a day on reading and recreation. If Mr. Smith spent less hours on reading and recreation, and didn't have to travel so far, he would have the time in which to work.

(If you cannot answer, check here..........)

6. On a certain day at Belmont race track, three prominent horse players were each using a different betting system.

System A ....Norm Lessing, the well-known plunger, bet $100 on the first race, $110 on the second, $120 on the third—intending to lift each bet by $10 in like fashion until he struck a winner.

System B ....James Marden, a more cautious player, bet as follows:
$10 on the first race

$15 on the second race

$30 on the third race, and so on—his system being to make each bet total all amounts previously lost, plus $5.

System C ....Benjy Parelli, former jockey, bet this way:

$10 on the first race

$10 on the second race

$40 on the third race, and so on—intending to keep doubling his bets until hitting a winner.

Which system required the least initial capital, if the better wanted to be sure to last through the day's card of seven races?

(If you cannot answer, check here..........)

Your Score . . . . .
Average Score: 8

SUPERIOR (UPPER TEN PER CENT)   0
GOOD (NEXT TWENTY PER CENT)   2–4
FAIR   (NEXT THIRTY PER CENT)   6–8
POOR (LOWEST FORTY PER CENT) 10–12

23. Are You Decisive?

THE inclination to make decisions on the spur of the moment is a handicap in most walks of life, and is fatal in some—science, for instance, which calls for suspended judgment and patience until all available facts add up.

Yet there are occasions enough when spot decisions must be made though we would rather suspend judgment; when indecision is a worse sin than a wrong decision. At such times we are like a swimmer lost out of sight of land. If he remains in the same spot endlessly debating with himself about the direction in which to strike out, sooner or later he will drown. But if he does strike out, in no matter which direction, there is some chance at least that he might reach shore.

The thing is that while we may be able to exercise fairly good judgment when given ample time to look at all sides of a situation, what happens when time is too short for such examination? Do we shilly-shally and waver? Or do we have the nerve and gumption to act decisively should action be indicated? And above all, when we find ourselves in such a spot do we merely guess—or do we keep sufficient presence of mind to make the best of the limited time or limited facts at our disposal? For swift judgment need not be snap judgment!

Strictly speaking, this challenging little test examines only a minute facet of what your behavior pattern might be under such stresses as those here discussed. It presents only one of the almost infinite number of "quick decision" situation-types encountered in life, many involving factors wholly different from those significant here. Yet the tasks which follow do tell you whether you act with more or less decisiveness and accuracy than others under like circumstances.

Part One:
DIRECTIONS—Decide which rows in each example add up to the three largest sums, and place a check next to these rows.
You will not have time to actually add all the rows. Either make the best guess you can, or add as many rows as you have time for on the chance that this will give you at least some answers likely to be correct.

TIME LIMIT: 2 MINUTES

DO NOT INSPECT EXAMPLES BEFORE BEGINNING TEST

Example I:
A. 1 2 3 4 5 6 7

B. 1 1 2 3 4 5 8

C. ..✗...7 6 5 4 3 2 1

D. 2 3 7 5 6 8 6

E. 2 3 4 5 6 6 7

F. 1 1 1 7 7 7 1

G. 2 8 3 4 5 6 8

H. 2 1 1 3 4 5 8

Example II:
A. 1 1 1 1 5 5 5

B. 1 5 1 5 1 5 1

C. 1 6 4 6 5 1 5

D. ......5 6 4 6 0 1 1 ✎

E. 6 1 1 5 5 4 0

F. 1 2 0 5 6 4 1

G. 1 5 3 6 7 5 1

H. ..✗...1 7 3 3 1 6 5

Example III:
A. 1 5 7 9 8 3 2

B. 9 0 3 6 7 2 1

C. 8 8 9 5 3 6 1

D. 4 5 6 4 5 3 9

E. 6 9 3 2 1 9 9

F. 5 4 1 2 8 3 8

G. ..✗...1 9 8 8 7 5 6

H. 5 6 7 6 5 8 7

125

Part Two:

DIRECTIONS—Decide which three rows contain the most letters, and place a check next to these rows. You will not have time to actually count the letters, but guess as shrewdly as you can.

TIME LIMIT: 30 SECONDS

Example IV:

1. ...... BBBBB BBBBB BBBBBB
2. ...... BWBWBWB BWBWBWB
3. ...... WWWWWW WWWWWW
4. ...... OOOOO OOOOOO OOOOO
5. ...... IIIIIII IIIIII IIIIII IIIIIII
6. ...... VOVOVOVOVOVO VOVOVOVO
7. ...... IIIIII IIII IIIII IIII IIIII
8. ...... WIWIWIWIWI WIWIW
9. ...... VIII VIIII VIIII VIII VIIII VIII

Part Three:

DIRECTIONS—Each circle is divided into sections. Check the two circles which are divided into the greatest number of sections. You will not have time to actually count the sections, but guess as shrewdly as you can.

TIME LIMIT: 30 SECONDS

Example V:

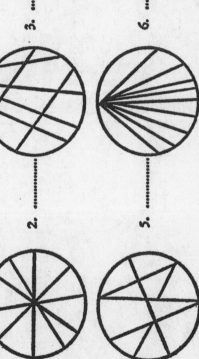

SUPERIOR (UPPER TEN PER CENT)   0–22

GOOD (NEXT TWENTY PER CENT)   23–31

FAIR   (NEXT THIRTY PER CENT)   32–41

POOR (LOWEST FORTY PER CENT)   42–77

24. Are You Thorough?

How often have we heard genius defined as "an infinite capacity for taking pains!" While not as simple as all that, genius does require enough intensity to assure thorough performance of a complex task down to the last detail. Many an otherwise gifted person falls short of genius because he lacks thoroughness. And less endowed folks sometimes come through with surprising successes simply because such tasks as they do perform, they perform thoroughly.

But a trick of genius is the precise selection of just those tasks which are most pertinent to the goal in mind, and complete concentration on these even to the neglect of less important ones. For with genius as with the rest of us, time is often too short to give every job painstaking attention; nor does every job merit such attention. So what usually counts is this: can you devote to a task the care it properly deserves—enough to get results, yet not so much as to become mere fussiness or repetitious thinking?

Test yourself in this regard by taking the quiz below.

DIRECTIONS—Accuracy is more important than speed in this case. Carefully count the dots in the designated areas, and write your answers on the blank lines at the left of each question.
TIME LIMIT: 3 MINUTES

How many dots are there—
1. ......In the square—but not in the triangle, circle or rectangle?
2. ......In the circle—but not in the triangle, square or rectangle?
3. ......In the triangle—but not in the circle, square or rectangle?

4. ......In the rectangle—but not in the triangle, circle or square?

5. ......Common to the triangle and circle—but not in the rectangle or square?

6. ......Common to the square and triangle—but not in the rectangle or circle?

7. ......Common to the square and circle—but not in the triangle or rectangle?

8. ......Common to the square and rectangle—but not in the circle or triangle?

9. ......Common to the triangle and rectangle—but not in the circle?

10. ......Common to the circle, square, triangle and rectangle?

Your Score . . . . .
Average Score: 5
SUPERIOR (UPPER TEN PER CENT)   0–2
EXCELLENT (NEXT TEN PER CENT)   3–4
GOOD (NEXT TWENTY PER CENT)   5–6
FAIR   (NEXT TWENTY PER CENT)   7–8
POOR (LOWEST FORTY PER CENT)   9–20

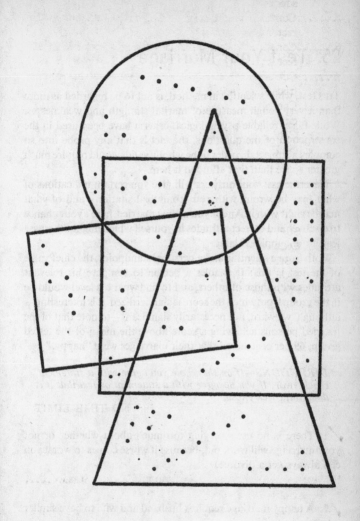

25. Test Your Marriage

THIS test, while scientific in method, is not to be regarded as more than a very rough measure of marital strength and weaknesses. While fairly reliable psychological criteria have been used in the construction of the questions, the fact is that any probe into so complex a subject, in order to be wholly valid, would require much greater space than that afforded it here.

Nevertheless, your answers will give you certain indications of what may be wrong with your connubial sitation—and of what maybe right with it. And if you are *not* married, here's your chance to discover and correct attitudes in yourself which might otherwise lead to unhappiness later.

Both from a scientific and a personal standpoint, the chief value of the test is this: It enables a person to compare his relevant attitudes with those of others, and to find what his level would be in the group from which the score is standardized. It is interesting— although, we warn, not necessarily significant—to note that of the married persons achieving a score above the mean of the tested group, 69 per cent stated that their marriages were "happy."

DIRECTIONS—If on the whole you agree with a statement, check TRUE. *If you disagree with a statement or feel that it is doubtful, check* FALSE.

NO TIME LIMIT

1. There is no use worrying too much about whether or not your marriage will work out, because if worse comes to worst you can always get a divorce.

TRUE......... FALSE........

2. A happy marriage requires husband and wife to have similar interests.

TRUE......... FALSE........

132

✗ 3. A happy marriage requires economic security.

TRUE..✓..... FALSE........

✗ 4. A woman is incapable of as intense a physical love as a man.

TRUE........ FALSE..✓.....

✗ 5. After a number of years of marriage, the attraction between husband and wife is bound to weaken.

TRUE..✓..... FALSE........

✓ 6. A man or woman of forty cannot be as attractive as a boy or girl of twenty.

TRUE........ FALSE.✓......

✓ 7. A man and woman cannot be close friends in the true sense of the word.

TRUE........ FALSE.✓......

✓ 8. Unless strong sex attraction persists between husband and wife, their marriage will generally go on the rocks sooner or late.

TRUE........ FALSE.✓......

✓ 9. To be really considerate, and in order not to make a mockery of love, husband and wife should set apart certain definite times for the sex acts.

TRUE........ FALSE..✓.....

✗ 10. It is all right for a person to dally with someone other than his marriage partner, as long as his or her affection and interest do not become involved.

TRUE........ FALSE.✓......

✓ 11. Marriages are happiest when one partner is always willing to acquiesce in the wishes of the other.

TRUE........ FALSE.✓......

133

✓ 12. A couple should not have intercourse more than once a week.

TRUE......... FALSE...✓.....

✓ 13. Children do more to hurt a marriage than to help it.

TRUE......... FALSE..✓......

✓ 14. An erring wife is more at fault than an erring husband.

TRUE......... FALSE..✓......

✓ 15. It is possible for a man to love two women at the same time, or for a woman to love two men at the same time.

TRUE......... FALSE.✓......

✓ 16. Marriages are generally happiest when husband and wife entertain as few friends and relatives as possible.

TRUE......... FALSE.✓......

✓ 17. The more a couple stays at home instead of going around to parties and affairs, the more chance they have to be happy.

TRUE......... FALSE.✓......

✓ 18. Love is a game.

TRUE......... FALSE.✓......

✗ 19. Love is a deadly serious matter.

TRUE...✓.... FALSE.........

✓ 20. For a truly happy marriage, the man should be able to make himself helpful around the house in such matters as fixing shelves or leaky faucets—and the woman should be able to cook good, wholesome meals.

TRUE......... FALSE.✓......

✓ 21. Husband and wife should always spend their vacations together.

TRUE......... FALSE.✓......

22. If husband and wife want to spend an evening or two away from each other occasionally, it's perfectly all right.

TRUE.. ✓.... FALSE........

23. Marriage is noble in a sense, because (check one):
a. It is sanctified by God..........
b. It insures continuation of the race..........
✓c. It can provide ideal companionship between man and woman... ✓.....

24. In most really happy marriages, the husband keeps business affairs out of the home and does not discuss them with his wife.

TRUE........ FALSE. ✓......

25. If a wife achieves greater social, professional or economic success than the husband the marriage eventually becomes unhappy.

TRUE........ FALSE. ✓......

Your Score .....
Average Score: 16
✓SUPERIOR (UPPER TEN PER CENT)   21–25
  GOOD (NEXT TWENTY PER CENT)   18–20
  FAIR   (NEXT THIRTY PER CENT)   16–17
  POOR (LOWEST FORTY PER CENT)   0–15

135

26. Can You Handle People?

TESTS intended to search our executive talent often includes scales that probe interpersonal attitudes. The attitudes at issue have to do with getting customers, underlings and colleagues to see things your way, and therefore do things your way. These same attitudes are useful not only to the business executive, however. They are important weapons in the arsenal of the professional man, the salesman or any other person whose work requires him to deal directly with individuals or small groups.

To handle larger groups—that is, to act as a "leader"—does not seem to call for the same attributes and attitudes obviously valuable in handling individuals. Despite continuing and exhaustive investigation by sociometrists and psychometrists, the qualities that determine group leadership remain obscure.

It is known, for example, that a group's "natural" leader may be one of the most popular persons in that group—but it is also known that frequently he is one of the least popular. The leader in one situation may be discarded for another if a new situation arises. Clubwomen may select a president on grounds that her intelligence and persuasiveness surpass their own, or reject her on that very account.

While studies concerned with group leadership turn up results often contradictory, inconsistent and confusing, the picture is less muddled in the area of person-to-person relationships. Here certain attitudes have emerged as fairly reliable indications of at least a latent power to lead and influence people individually, or in assemblies of two or three—too small to show involved group dynamics.

To be sure, leading and handling people in the business world may be accomplished in a number of ways. Some executives, not too many, function by inspiring and stimulating those around them. Others find effectiveness in cracking the whip—putting fear into

136

the hearts of subordinates, coercing superiors, threatening suppliers.

Yet such courses are not the ones most frequently relied on. Usually the persons successful in their business or professional contacts are neither inspirational figures nor martinets. Rather, they have simply acquired convincing techniques of word, manner and approach. These in turn stem from attitudes investigated in the quiz that follows.

DIRECTIONS—Answers each question as indicated. Do not guess, but do not be over-cautious. If you do not wish to make a choice, check the appropriate square.

TIME LIMIT: 4 MINUTES

1. A good vocabulary is often the mark of a superior person. Words like "quotidian"—which means "occurring daily"—are not only highly impressive but often more apt and accurate. Assuming that you are addressing a Doctor of Philosophy, exceptionally cultured and a master of several languages including English, which phrase would you consider more effective in putting across your idea? (*Check one.*)

✓ A ...."It happens day after day."

B ...."It is a quotidian occurrence."

C ...."It occurs frequently."

NO CHOICE ☐

✗ 2. Generally speaking, which of the following sentences is to be preferred? (*Check one.*)

A ....I happened to be in the neighborhood, so I thought I'd drop in and discuss things.

B ....✓...I came here especially to talk to you about this matter.

NO CHOICE ☐

3. You are an employer, and one of your men comes to you with some small idea for increasing efficiency. You had already

thought of the idea and are preparing to put it into effect. Which of the following actions would it be better to take? (*Check one.*)

✓ A... ✓ ...Tell the employee that you have already thought of the idea, but do appreciate his suggestion.

B ....Say nothing about your prior conception, but simply praise the employee for his cooperation.

NO CHOICE ☐

✓ 4. A woman comes into your newly opened shoe store to buy a pair of pumps. You have difficulty fitting her because her right foot is larger than her left, and you find it necessary to explain that to her. Fill in the best words:

"Madam, your. left ...foot is. smaller than your. right."

NO CHOICE ☐

5. You are manager of a department store. An irate customer rushes into your office and pours out an impassioned complaint. You quickly realize she is in the wrong. What should your first step in the matter be? (*Check one.*)

A .... ✓ ...Try to appreciate how she arived at her point of view, however erroneous it may be, and show some sympathy.

B ....Let her know gently that she is laboring under a misapprehension, and that the mistake is hers, not the store's.

✓ C ....Tell her that you have no authority and to get satisfaction, if it be due, she will have to go at once to the store's Complaint Department, or to a minor executive on your staff.

NO CHOICE ☐

✓ 6. When trying to get a stubborn associate to proceed with your idea or suggestion, you should do either of the following. (*Check one.*)

A .... ✓ ..If possible, try to present the idea in such a way that he feels it emerges at least partly, from his brain.

B ....Make certain that you get full credit for the idea.

NO CHOICE ☐

7. You know that one of your prospective customers collects butterflies. Although you are seeing him on a purely business matter, you produce a butterfly specimen and say, "By the way, Mr. Jones, I've heard you're an expert on butterflies. My youngster caught this one, and I've saved it to ask you what kind it is." Which of the following would be more likely to result? (*Check one.*)

A ....The customer would consider you presumptuous and out of order.

✓ B ...✓...The customer would be more favorably disposed toward you.

NO CHOICE ☐

8. Your department has a series of tasks to perform which entails a number of complicated details. Being a busy executive who has risen through the ranks, you know that you can execute those details much better than any member of your staff. Therefore, you should do which of the following? (*Check one.*)

A ....Take the time to handle in full every detail personally.

✓ B ...✓....Plan to delegate many of the details to subordinates.

NO CHOICE ☐

9. You realize that you and a young subordinate were short-changed thirty cents at a restaurant you left about ten minutes ago. You get a substantial salary and your time is pretty valuable. Which should you do? (*Check one.*)

A ....Since it is not the money but the principle of the thing that is involved, you should go back to the restaurant, put in a complaint, and if possible collect what is rightfully due you.

✓ B ...✓....Forget the whole thing.

C ....Send back the subordinate to put in the complaint and claim the money.

NO CHOICE ☐

10. Lack of space obliges you to place the desk of a high-powered traffic specialist next to the desks of the typist pool. She performs her job beautifully for $7,500 per year, and has been with the firm since it started. But she comes and goes at all hours, takes unauthorized coffee breaks, dresses sloppily, never has a neat desk —thus setting a bad example for the fine typists. Working for $60 per week each, these girls are especially impressionable since they are fresh out of business school. You should therefore take action as follows. (*Check one*).

✗ A ...✓....Fire the traffic specialist.

 B ....Fire the typists if they step out of line, because girls from business school are a lot easier to replace than skilled traffic personnel.

NO CHOICE ☐

SUPERIOR (UPPER TEN PER CENT) 27–30
GOOD (NEXT TWENTY PER CENT) 21–24
✓FAIR   (NEXT THIRTY PER CENT) 16–19
POOR (LOWEST FORTY PER CENT)   0–15

27. Can You Assess Situations?

Too often, people fail to solve business or personal problems because of inability to assess the relative weights of pertinent factors. Or they may simply be unable to recognize the pertinent, and so waste time and energy on irrelevant considerations.

The first law in arriving at problem solutions, then, is to analyze all factors in terms not only of relative importance but also of relative pertinence. This test gives you a chance to demonstrate your virtuosity at such analysis.

On any job, and in every profession, facility in assessment of data supplied by the senses and the brain is vitally helpful. The speed of such assessment, however, may be equally important. For this reason, there is a time limitation put on the scale that follows.

DIRECTIONS—If on the whole you agree with a statement, check TRUE. If you disagree with a statement or feel that it is doubtful, check FALSE.

TIME LIMIT: 4 MINUTES

1. A business employs five hundred non-skilled laborers earning $80 each per week, and ten executives earning $180 per week. The manager figures out that if he lowers the pay of each employee by 5%, he will save the company more than $100,000 annually.

Of course, a wholesale pay-cut would incur the risk of many employees quitting. On the other hand, the manager knows that one non-skilled laborer is about as good as another and plenty in the vicinity are willing to work for $70 per week. He also knows where to get perfectly good executives for $150 per week. He should, therefore, institute the pay decrease of 5% for all employees.

TRUE ☐   FALSE ☐

2. You drop a coin into a pay telephone. You make your call, and hang up, whereupon the dime is returned to you. Rather than keep this ten cents, you should reimburse the telephone company.

TRUE ☐   FALSE ☐

3. Better to give to an organized charity than to a beggar, even though the charity devotes half of all donations to payment of its own expenses.

TRUE ☐   FALSE ☐

4. A horse with a broken leg should be shot, for although curing the leg is possible, it is a long expensive process, and hard on the horse—unless, of course, anesthetics and pain-killers are used.

TRUE ☐   FALSE ☐

5. Baked clams should not be ordered in a restaurant because the clams go into the oven alive.

TRUE ☐   FALSE ☐

6. Lobsters should not be eaten in the home because they must be cooked alive, which is torture for them.

TRUE ☐   FALSE ☐

7. Highway billboards contribute much to the national business income. Nevertheless, they should be banned, because they mar the natural beauty of the countryside.

TRUE ☐   FALSE ☐

8. If you have time, better to haggle with a tradesman than to let him overcharge you.

TRUE ☐   FALSE ☐

9. You know that waiters depend on tips for a living. In a strange town, you go into a restaurant and get very bad service. Nevertheless, you should be tolerant enough to leave your usual tip instead of reducing it.

TRUE ☐   FALSE ☐

10. You go into a restaurant you frequent every day. Your usually competent waiter gives you bad service on this occasion. Nevertheless, you should leave him your customary generous tip, because if you reduced it to show your displeasure, most likely you would get even worse service on following days.

TRUE ☐   FALSE ☐

11. You are lunching in a restaurant you frequent almost daily. Your usually indifferent waiter gives you exceptionally swift, competent and cheerful service. But you should not show appreciation by leaving more than your customary tip, as this would establish a precedent quite expensive if continued—or result in poor service if discontinued—and in any case, it is to be expected of a professional waiter that he give good, cheerful service.

TRUE ☐   FALSE ☐

12. Leaving a bank after you have cashed a traveler's check, you discover that the teller has given you ten dollars too much. Assume that the bank, all personnel, and the company that issued the check are insured against losses, and you know as much. In such a case, you might as well keep the money, since you did not steal it and it would deprive nobody.

TRUE ☐   FALSE ☐

SUPERIOR (UPPER FIVE PER CENT)   0–2
GOOD   (NEXT FIFTEEN PER CENT)   3–7
FAIR   (NEXT THIRTY PER CENT)   8–13
POOR (LOWEST FIFTY PER CENT)   14–24

28. Are You Ingenious?

MAYBE there is nothing new under the sun. But new ways of combining and utilizing existing objects or concepts keep the architect, engineer, scientist, inventor and even the artist in business. To make new shapes out of old, to evolve new ideas by altering and blending old ones, involves first of all an analysis—a breakdown into parts, forms and properties. This is followed by a synthesis—putting together those fractions into a new whole with altered characteristics.

The analysis-synthesis approach is common chiefly among trained thinkers. The creative person, particularly in the arts and crafts, frequently dispenses with analysis and concentrates on synthesis, taking given materials or ideas and recombining them into new forms by the trial-and-error method.

While the trials may be made in the person's head rather than on paper or a sewing machine, they are not the same thing as analysis. The latter makes possible swifter, more flexible and possibly more accurate synthesis in complex creative situations.

Thus, the end result would be the same in any one item of the following test whether you proceeded by first analyzing the shapes or put them together into the new form by means of trial and error. But your over-all score would suffer unless you preceded each synthesis by a bit of shrewd analysis, if only because you would lose time in finding the solutions.

This test in essence resembles *12. Are You Inventive?* but is of a greater order of difficulty; in fact, it is perhaps the most difficult test in the book. A high score tends to indicate aptitude for pursuits involving creativity, organized thinking, and the factor of intelligence implied in grasp of spacial relationships—but not necessarily involving verbal skills.

144

DIRECTIONS—In each of the ten problems, the separate pieces can be put together to form the large, dark figure. Draw free-hand lines on the large figure to indicate how it could be made up of the pieces. You may measure with your pencil or fingers only.

TIME LIMIT: 25 MINUTES

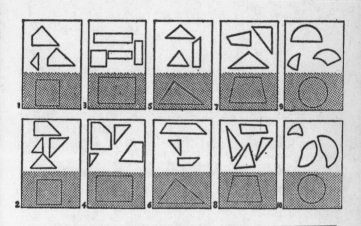

SUPERIOR (UPPER TEN PER CENT)   13–16
GOOD (NEXT TWENTY PER CENT)   9–12
FAIR   (NEXT THIRTY PER CENT)   5–8
POOR (LOWEST FORTY PER CENT)   0–4

JOB APTITUDES

29. Have You A Mechanical Bent?

MECHANICAL aptitude can mean the knack of handling tools, machinery and physical objects generally. But the fellow who designs an engine—though unable to build or assembly it himself—none the less can be said to show a distinct mechanical flair.

In other words, there is a level at which the tool may be an instrument, even a formula; where appreciation of mechanical principles is the big thing rather than the trick of manipulating a monkey-wrench.

As it stands, the test below concerns itself with this second interpretation of mechanical inclination. Manual and motor skills are not considered. Some clue is sought, rather, to your ingenuity with spaces and forces, and your grasp of mechanical phenomena. Visualization and spatial reasoning, tested elsewhere, also contribute to your score.

But as might be expected, the factors tested are likewise characteristic of the person coming under our first definition of mechanical aptitude. The man superior at tool manipulation, say. The man able to skillfully assemble or repair mechanical devices. To furnish some indication of your potential in this direction a separate score is provided, weighted to stress manual and motor aptitudes.

DIRECTIONS—In each example, check the phrase which correctly completes the statement. Do not guess.

NO TIME LIMIT

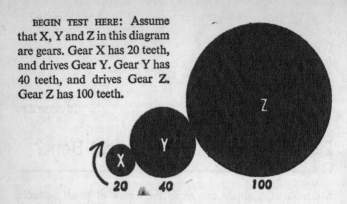

BEGIN TEST HERE: Assume that X, Y and Z in this diagram are gears. Gear X has 20 teeth, and drives Gear Y. Gear Y has 40 teeth, and drives Gear Z. Gear Z has 100 teeth.

1. If X turns in the direction shown by the arrow, Y will move in the:
(a)......Same direction as the arrow.
(b)......Opposite direction to the arrow.
(c)......Partly in the same direction as the arrow, and partly counter-clockwise.

2. If X turns in the direction shown by the arrow, Z will move in the:
(a)......Same direction as the arrow.
(b)......Opposite direction to the arrow.
(c)......Partly in the same direction as the arrow, and partly counter-clockwise.

3. If Z makes a complete turn, X will make:
(a)......1/5 of a turn.
(b)......5 turns.
(c)......$1\frac{1}{4}$ turns.

4. If X makes a complete turn, Z will make:
(a)......1/5 of a turn.
(b)......5 turns.
(c)......$1\frac{1}{4}$ turns.

150

5. If X makes a complete turn, how many turns will Y make?

(a)......2 turns.

(b)......$\frac{1}{2}$ turn.

(c)......20 turns.

6. If a fourth gear is inserted between X and Y, this will cause Z to turn:

(a)......Faster.

(b)......Neither faster nor slower.

(c)......It depends on the size of the fourth gear.

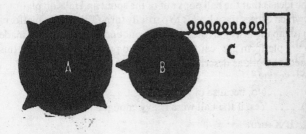

7. Examine the diagram above. Wheel A has 4 teeth and Wheel B has 1 tooth. When not being made to turn, B is snapped back to the original position by the pull of the steel spring C. Therefore:

(a)......Since A meshes with B, and since B cannot turn continuously because of the spring C, it follows that A cannot turn continuously.

(b)......If Wheel A turned clockwise more than once, then either B would stretch the spring too far and so force the apparatus to stop, or the spring would break under the tension.

(c)......A could keep turning, causing the tooth on B to move down and up 4 times to each revolution of A.

151

8. Take a look at the peculiar machine below, probably invented by Rube Goldberg. It is shown in starting position.

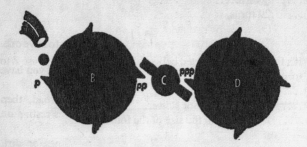

The idea is that the ball pops out of the spout and falls on platform *p*, which causes the wheel B to partially turn. This causes platform *pp* to tap the heavy pivoted beam C, one end of which is thus made to tap platform *ppp*, causing wheel D to partially turn. Could this machine work as described?

(a)......No.

(b)......No, because of friction.

(c)......Yes, if the ball were heavy enough.

9. You want to get a stubborn screw out of your wall. It is already half out, but you have no screwdriver with which to finish the job. The best substitute tool is:

      (a)......A coin.

      (b)......A table knife.

      (c)......A penknife.

      (d)......Pliers.

10. You want to remove the nut from a rusty bolt sticking out of your stove. Since you have no pliers, you should use:

      (a)......A piece of wire looped around the nut.

      (b)......Scissors.

      (c)......A hammer.

      (d)......Your teeth.

11. You want to drive a nail into your closet wall, but have no hammer. You should use:
   - (a)......A knife handle.
   - (b)......A can opener.
   - (c)......Heavy pliers.
   - (d)......A riveting machine, if you happen to have one.

12. Your car has a flat rear tire on a country road, and you have no jack. You can change tires by:
   - (a)......Placing your spare tire on the road, then backing your car till the flat tire is resting on the spare tire.
   - (b)......Scraping together a pile of stones or dirt, placing your spare tire on the mound, then backing your car till the flat tire is resting on the spare—and proceeding from there.
   - (c)......Scraping together a pile of stones or dirt, then backing your car so that the rear axle climbs the mound.

13. A box nailed together is stronger than the same box glued together.
   - (a)......Of course.
   - (b)......Of course not.
   - (c)......Not necessarily.

14. The diagrams show 3 types of pulley arrangements. The pulleys weigh 1 pound each. The weights tip the scales at 500 pounds each. Check the arrangement which will require the least pull in the direction of the arrow in order to lift the weight.

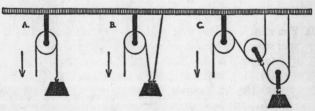

KNACK FOR HANDLING TOOLS
Your Score .....
Average Score: 193

SUPERIOR	(UPPER TEN PER CENT)	above 238
GOOD	(NEXT TWENTY PER CENT)	211–238
FAIR	(NEXT THIRTY PER CENT)	184–210
POOR	(LOWEST FORTY PER CENT)	0–183

MECHANICAL UNDERSTANDING
Your Score .....
Average Score: 125

SUPERIOR	(UPPER TEN PER CENT)	above 162
GOOD	(NEXT TWENTY PER CENT)	140–162
FAIR	(NEXT THIRTY PER CENT)	118–139
POOR	(LOWEST FORTY PER CENT)	0–117

30. Have You Pattern Skill?

WHEN you try for an industrial job today you may run into the type of test on the next page, which has become a great favorite with vocational counselors and personnel departments. It requires little mental effort and is amusing to take—but just what it measures is debatable.

As in simple serial and pursuit tests, a general *perception* factor affects the score you will get. But the more significant loading seems to lie with the *location* and *copying* factors brought to wide notice by MacQuarrie and others. (cf. *MacQuarrie Mechanical Ability* series, California Test Bureau.)

If we are to believe the claims sometimes made for tests of this kind, they can demonstrate predilection for an enormous variety of tasks. These range from wrapping and packing to making the spatial adjustments required in handling tools and assembling.

Illustrating the lengths to which such claims can go, a recent popular work on job guidance held that the pattern-copying test measures "creative lay-out" ability. How absurd! Obviously, copying is the direct negation of creation.

So a warning is in order. While the pattern-copying test can be plausibly associated with ability in many industrial tasks, a high score does not necessarily prove such ability. Nor does a low score disprove it. The fact is that significant correlations are scarce. However, the test is included here as an example of what you are likely to meet if you want work in our larger factories and assembly plants.

DIRECTIONS—One circle in each pair contains a pattern of X-marks. Duplicate the pattern by making X's on corresponding points of the second circle For example:

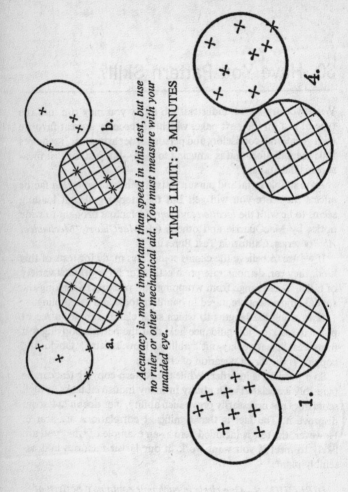

Accuracy is more important than speed in this test, but use
no ruler or other mechanical aid. You must measure with your
unaided eye.

TIME LIMIT: 3 MINUTES

156

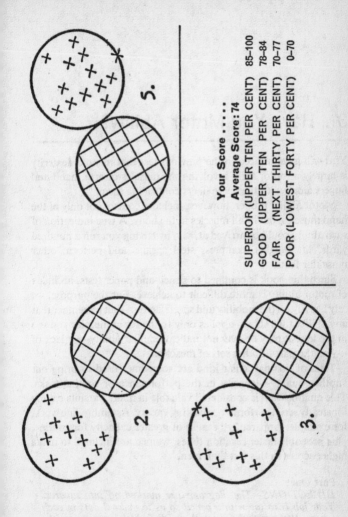

Your Score . . . . . .

Average Score: 74

SUPERIOR	(UPPER TEN PER CENT)	85-100
GOOD	(UPPER TEN PER CENT)	78-84
FAIR	(NEXT THIRTY PER CENT)	70-77
POOR	(LOWEST FORTY PER CENT)	0-70

31. Have You Motor Ability?

You will have noticed in the previous test that manual dexterity is largely a motor skill, involving the muscles of arm, hand and fingers along with the nerve fibers controlling them.

Motor ability proper, however, includes control not only of the hand muscles, but of all muscles in the body. A true indication of such ability could be arrived at, say, by having you run a hundred yards, lift weights, compress steel springs and perform other muscular feats.

Since this book is confined to pencil-and-paper tests, an index of motor ability is more difficult to achieve. For the purpose, we rely heavily on the mobility and speed factors—but remember that any ability thus shown applies only to the set of muscles you use in the test. It may or may not indicate similar ability—or lack of it—on the part of other sets of muscles.

Tests of this particular kind are sometimes used to bring out another quality—tenacity in the performance of routine tasks. This qualification is considered valuable in many pursuits calling for steady serial performance lacking variety. Assembly-line work, for example. Apparently because of greater capacity for routine, plus probable faster reaction times, women are inclined to make higher scores in this test than men.

Part One:
DIRECTIONS—The diagrams are marked off into squares. Your job is to tap with a pencil so as to make 2 dots in each square. Work with the greatest speed of which you are capable.
                              TIME LIMIT: 2 MINUTES

Part Two:

DIRECTIONS—By tapping with your pencil, place 1 dot in each circle. Work with your utmost speed.

TIME LIMIT: 3 MINUTES

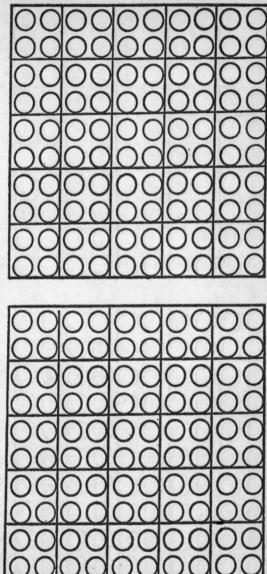

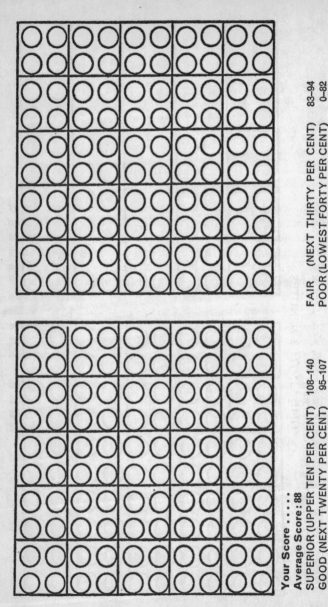

Your Score . . . . .
Average Score: 88
SUPERIOR (UPPER TEN PER CENT)   108–140
GOOD (NEXT TWENTY PER CENT)   95–107
FAIR (NEXT THIRTY PER CENT)   83–94
POOR (LOWEST FORTY PER CENT)   0–82

32. Are You Dextrous?

In our machine age, the "manual dexterity" so often tested for by vocational psychologists is apt to mean skill in the swift, precise performance of simple hand movements. Although such skill is unquestionably valuable in a mass production society, it bears little resemblance to the more complex dexterity important in the days when men built their own huts and made their own shoes.

Like most performance tests, those in current use to measure manual dexterity lend themselves well to standardization. On the other hand, they often tend to confuse mobility and accuracy. One man can place more dots in a given area for instance. Another man can make more dots in a given time. Which is the more dextrous?

Our own dexterity test places the emphasis on accuracy, on the theory that the person who fumbles cannot properly be called dextrous. Also, an innovation is added—holding the pencil by its end—which introduces elements of a somewhat broader hand control than that demonstrated in most tests of the kind.

Part One:
DIRECTIONS—To take this test you need a pencil 7 inches long. Grasp the pencil by its unsharpened end and hold it at arm's length, with your arm stretched stiffly in front of you. With your arm and hand in this position, place an X in each circle and a dot in each square. The X must not extend over the limits of the circle.

Practice the sample test below, performing it once with your right hand and once with your left hand.

Now take the test on the next page, remembering that accuracy is more important than speed.

TIME LIMIT: 1 MINUTE

USE LEFT HAND:

USE RIGHT HAND:

Part Two:

DIRECTIONS—With arm, hand and pencil in the same position as in Part One, draw a continuous line over all X's and under all O's in each line. For example:

20. X O X X O O O O X X X X O O O O

Use right or left hand, whichever you prefer. Be careful to draw your line in such fashion that it does not touch any of the letters.

TIME LIMIT: 2 MINUTES

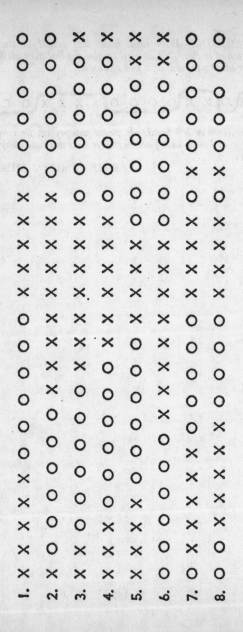

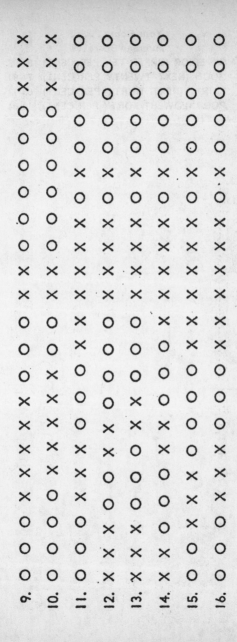

Your Score . . . . .
Average Score: 69

SUPERIOR (UPPER TEN PER CENT) 81–98
GOOD (NEXT TWENTY PER CENT) 74–80
FAIR   (NEXT THIRTY PER CENT) 65–73
POOR (LOWEST FORTY PER CENT) 0–64

ANSWER SECTION

Answers and Scoring

ARBITRARY rankings such as SUPERIOR, POOR and so on have been assigned in this book to fixed percentages of the whole group. The limits of each ranking are called *percentiles* by psychologists. The percentile limits are always at a certain precise distance from the group mean—a distance which psychologists generally measure in units of *Standard Deviation*, or SD.

For those interested, the SD values for each test are included in the Answer Section. As for the number of SD's represented by the various ladder rankings above or below the mean, these are as follows:

Upper 10 per cent.... +1.30 SD or more
Next   10 per cent.... + .85 to 1.29 SD
Next   10 per cent.... + .55 to .84 SD
Next   10 per cent.... + .25 to .54 SD
Next   10 per cent.....00 (mean) to .24 SD
Next   10 per cent.... —.25 to —.01 SD
Low   40 per cent.... Less than —.25 SD

These values, of course, apply only to tests whose results demonstrably conform to standard Gaussian curve dimensions. In cases where the distribution of answers is bunched at the high and low ends of the curve, the Standard Deviation and Probable Error are omitted. They are likewise omitted where the number of test items is judged insufficient for a significant curve.

* * *

It should be noted that while different tests may purport to measure the same characteristics, they yield scores which have only a relative significance to each other.

Thus, the maximum I. Q. which can be achieved on one test may be about 140 (*Dominion Series, etc.*), while on others it may go as high as 170 or more (*Dearborn, Series II*).

The actual degree of intelligence is indicated not so much by the I.Q. itself as by the position of the I.Q. in the scores achieved by those taking the particular test. The adult who scores 170 on one type of test is no more intelligent than the man who scores 140 on another type of test if in both cases the scores were in equivalent percentile rankings of the respective groups.

The scoring ladder at the end of the test, giving the percentile group into which your score falls, is therefore a more reliable index of intelligence than the I.Q. figure alone.

1. What's Your I.Q.?

1(2), 2(1), 3(27), 4(3), 5(12), 6(F), 7(F), 8(9), 9(T), 10(1), 11(b), 12(4), 13(3), 14(4), 15(3), 16(4), 17(15), 18(77), 19(3), 20(4).

21(4), 22(2), 23(K), 24(8), 25(I), 26(Q), 27(c), 28(F), 29(9), 30(D), 31(T), 32(c), 33(d), 34(17), 35(0), 36(c), 37(6), 38(3), 39(7), 40(4).

41(I), 42(9), 43(3), 44(27), 45(4), 46(21), 47(c), 48(54), 49(5), 50(1), 51(5), 52(90), 53(7), 54(10), 55(4), 56(60), 57(2), 58(c), 59(1), 60(3).

61(4), 62(4), 63(1), 64(4), 65(3), 66($8\frac{1}{2}$), 67(3), 68(1140), 69(2), 70(5), 71(5), 72(4), 73(30), 74(SRQ).

75(4-10-2-8-10-8), 76(200), 77(2), 78(3), 79(550), 80(41), 81(4), 82(6), 83(12), 84(d), 85(2), 86(2), 87(15), 88(2/5), 89(5), 90(T).

Give yourself 1 point for each correct answer. Total points is your score.

SD:16.5   PE:11

2. Are You Adaptable?

(1) 8,   (2) 7,   (3) B,   (4) 12,   (5) T,   (6) C,
(7) 81, (8) 12, (9) [symbol], (10) 2, (11) I, (12) / ,
(13) [figure] ,   (14) 140,   (15) C,   (16) 8,   (17) *,
(18) *****,   (19) 15,   (20) V,   (21) [symbol] ,   (22)
[symbol] , (23) [clock symbol] ,   (24) W,   (25) F,   (26) 8,   (27) P,
(28) 6,   (29) f,   (30) G.

Give yourself 3 points for each correct answer.

SD:13.5   PE:9

3. Do You Really See?

PART ONE:
  Reading from left to right: Row One: 1st and 6th figures. Row Two: 1st and 4th figures. Row Three: 2nd and 6th figures. Row Four: 4th and 6th figures. Row Five: 2nd and 5th figures. Row Six: 2nd and 6th figures. Row Seven: 2nd and 5th figures.

PART TWO:
  1—D, 2—S, 3—D, 4—S, 5—D, 6—D, 7—D, 8—S, 9—D, 10—D, 11—S, 12—D, 13—S, 14—D, 15—S, 16—D, 17—D, 18—D, 19—D, 20—D
  Mark yourself 1 point for each correct answer in Part One; 5 points for each correct answer in Part Two. Total points is your score.

SD:5   PE:3.4

4. Can You Concentrate?

There are 143 pairs adding up to 10.
Score yourself 1 point for each pair omitted or wrongly marked.
SD:13.8   PE:9.8

5. How's Your Memory?

Give yourself 1 point for each correct answer. Add the points in both parts for your score.

SD:4.7   PE:3

6. Do You Think Straight?

One) 1—T; *Two)* 1—F; *Three)* 1—F, 2—T; *Four)* 1—F; *Five)* 1—F, 2—T; *Six)* 1—F, 2—F, 3—T; *Seven)* 1—F; *Eight)* 1—T, 2—F; *Nine)* 1—F, 2—F, 3—T; *Ten)* 1—F, 2—T, 3—F; *Eleven)* 1—F, 2—F, 3—T

Twelve) 1—F, 2—F, 3—T; *Thirteen)* 1—F, 2—F, 3—T; *Fourteen)* 1—F, 2—F, 3—T; *Fifteen)* 1—T, 2—F, 3—F; *Sixteen)* 1—T, 2—F, 3—F; *Seventeen)* 1—F, 2—F, 3—T; *Eighteen)* 1—T, 2—F; *Nineteen)* 1—F, 2—F, 3—F; *Twenty)* 1—F, 2—F, 3—T

Give yourself 1 point for each wrong answer, and 1 point for each omitted answer. Add these points to obtain your score.

SD:7.7   PE:5

7. How Smart Are You?

PART ONE:

(1) 7, 13; (2) V, T; (3) G, M; (4) 200; (5) L; (6) 9, 15; (7) 1, 3, 243; (8) 11, 14; (9) 6, 54 or 9, 54; (10) 23, 30; (11) B, W, V; (12) 200

PART TWO:

Reading from left to right and from top to bottom—
A. 9-9-3, 3-9-9, 9-3-9
B. 9-9-9-7, 9-9-7-9, 7-9-9-9, 9-7-9-9
C. 9-8-9-8, 9-9-7-9, 8-9-9-8, 8-8-9-9

PART THREE:

1: DUCK 2: GULL 3: ROBIN 4: CROW 5: HEN 6: PIGEON
7: HAWK 8: OWL 9: PARROT 10: SPARROW 11: EAGLE
12: CHICKEN 13: BLUEBIRD 14: BLACKBIRD 15: STORK

PART FOUR:

1: COW 2: TIGER 3: HORSE 4: MONKEY 5: RABBIT 6: SQUIRREL 7: SHEEP 8: CAT 9: MOUSE 10: BUFFALO 11: CAMEL · 12: SKUNK 13: DONKEY 14: GORILLA 15: ELEPHANT 16: BEAR 17: LION

Credit yourself as follows:
2 points for each correct answer in Part One.
2 points for each correct answer in Part Two.
1 point for each correct answer in Part Three.
1 point for each correct answer in Part Four.
Total of all points is your score.

SD:10   PE:6.8

8. Have You Musical Talent?

1—a, 2—b, 3—a, 4—Pleasant, 5—Pleasant, 6—a, 7—a. 8— The notes should be C-E-G in any order, or C-E-A in any order, or B-flat combined with any two of the notes C-E-G. 9 and 10— your friend will tell you whether or not you are correct.
Give yourself 1 point for each correct answer.

9. A Head For Figures?

1) 8 2) 16 3) 55 4) 80c 5) 8 6) 43 7) $1\frac{1}{4}$ minutes, or 1 minute and 15 seconds, or 75 seconds 8) 63 9) 465 10) 20 11) 2/3 12) $14 13) $1\frac{1}{2}$ weeks or $10\frac{1}{2}$ days 14) YES 15) YES 16) 10 17) 3 P.M. 18) 24 19)

```
        7 9 5 4
      ×     6 9
     ─────────────
        7 1 5 8 6
    4 7 7 2 4
    ─────────────
    5 4 8 8 2 6
```

20) B—7, C—6, D—4, E—3, F—2

175

21)

$$
\begin{array}{r}
5\ C\ 4 \\
\times\ C\ 5 \\
\hline
2\ F\ A\ Y \\
A\ 1\ F\ 6\quad \\
\hline
A\ C\ 4\ 8\ Y
\end{array}
$$

A—2, C—4, F—7, Y—0

22) 55

You get 1 point for each correct answer.

SD:3.3   PE:2.3

10. Can You Look Ahead?

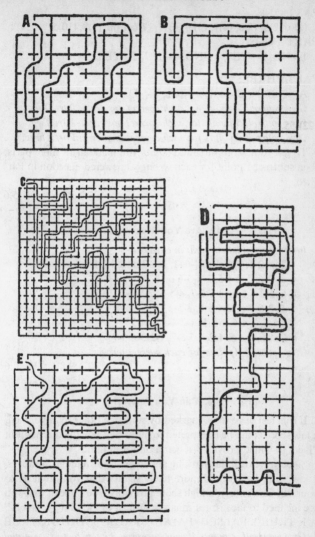

Give yourself 1 point for each correct answer.

11. Can You Visualize?

PART ONE:
(1)6, (2)5, (3)8, (4)7, (5)5, (6)11, (7)6, (8)6, (9)8, (10)5.

PART TWO:
1—NO, 2—YES, 3—NO, 4—NO, 5—YES.

PART THREE:
A—3, B—4, C—4, D—None, E—3.

Give yourself 2 points for each correct answer in Part One.
Give yourself 5 points for each correct answer in Part Two.
Give yourself 3 points for each correct answer in Part Three.

To get your score, first add points you made in all three parts, then subtract 1 point for each wrongly answered question in Part Two.

SD:8.3   PE:5.6

12. Are You Inventive?

Reading from left to right in each row—

A.   1-2 or 2-6, 5, 2-4-6, 4-6, 1, 2-6-7 or 2-4-5-6
B.   4, 3, 2-6, 1-2-4-5, 2-4-5-6 or 1-2-4-5, 3-4-5
C.   4-6, 2-3-5-6 or 2-4-6-7, 4-5-6, 2-5-6-7, 1-4-5
D.   1-5, 2-6-7 or 2-4-5-6, 3-5-6, 3-5, 1-2-4
E.   1-2-5-6, 2-4-6, 1-3-5, 1-2-4-5-6, 4-5
F.   4-6, 4-6, 1-3-5, 1-2-4-5-6-7, 1-2-3-4-5-7

Give yourself 3 points for each correct answer.

SD:9.8   PE:6.6

13. Can You Answer?

If this test were to be marked by someone other than yourself, a low score could be interpreted to mean that you make a habit of "lying to win approval"—a common social fault.

Since you do all the marking and are your own judge, however, a low score here would more likely signify that you often lie to yourself. Conversely, a high score probably would mean that you are inclined to face issues squarely instead of "kidding yourself."

1. TRUE 2. FALSE 3. FALSE 4. FALSE 5. TRUE 6. TRUE
7. *Give yourself 2 points if you answered TRUE to this item and*

178

FALSE to Item 11, or if you answered FALSE to this item and TRUE to Item 11. Otherwise give yourself no points.

8. FALSE 9. FALSE 10. FALSE 11. (See 7 above.) 12. *Give yourself 2 points if you answered TRUE to both this item and Item 21, or if you answered FALSE to both this item and Item 21. Otherwise give yourself no points.*

13. TRUE 14. *Give yourself 2 points if you answered TRUE to both this item and Item 20, or if you answered FALSE to both this item and Item 20. Otherwise give yourself no points.*

15. *Give yourself 3 points if you answered TRUE to this item, FALSE to Item 19, and TRUE to Item 24. Or give yourself 3 points if you answered FALSE to this item, TRUE to Item 19 and FALSE to Item 24. Otherwise give yourself no points.*

16. TRUE 17. FALSE 18. FALSE (No such word exists.) 19. (See 15 above.) 20. (See 14 above.) 21. (See 12 above.) 22. TRUE 23. TRUE 24. (See 15 above.) 25. TRUE

Give yourself 1 point for each correct answer, except as indicated above. Total points is your score.

14. Have You Esthetic Taste?

PART ONE:
Reading from left to right:
ROW ONE—2, ROW TWO—3, ROW THREE—3, ROW FOUR—1, ROW FIVE—3, ROW SIX—3, ROW SEVEN—3, ROW EIGHT—1, ROW NINE—1, ROW TEN—2
PART TWO:
1—b, 2—b, 3—a, 4—b, 5—b, 6—b, 7—b, 8—b, 9—b, 10—a
Give yourself 3 points for each correct answer in Part One; 2 points for each correct answer in Part Two.

SD:7.5   PE:5

15. Are You Artistic?

1. YES, 2. YES, 3. YES, 4. (a)NO (b)YES (c)YES

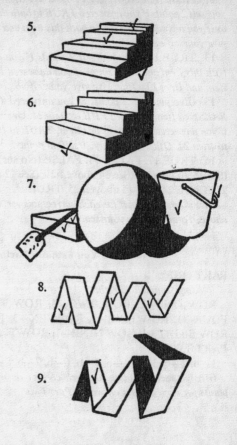

5.

6.

7.

8.

9.

10. (f), 11. (f), 12. (C), 13. None, 14 (a) YES (b) YES, 15. NO, 16. NO

In Items 5, 6, 7, 8, and 9, give yourself 1 point for each properly marked edge or surface. In the remaining Items, give yourself 1 point for each correct answer.

16. What's Your Art S–R?

The aim of this test is to measure the *degree* of your response to the given stimuli rather than just *how* you respond.

Hence you get 1 point for each word you listed, regardless of the drawing with which you associated that word.

SD:14   PE:9.4

17. Can You Succeed?

The one big quality essential to achievement in this life may be summed up in the word *reliability*! Unless you can be trusted—unless you can be dependable and honest in the things you do and in your relations with others—then eventually people will lose faith in you, just as you will lose it in yourself; and your life will hold more of failure than success.

So if you hit any target flush center once out of the five tries, we'll be charitable and put it down to accident.

But if you hit twice or more out of the five tries, you failed the test. For you must have opened your eyes—and therefore are unreliable!

18. Are You A Good Lover?

1. NO: Too much politeness maintains distance.

2. NO: There is no rule because individuals vary. The normal male no more desires a continually submissive clinging vine than does the average girl really desire a self-centered chest-thumper.

3. NO: Natural behavior, rather than artificial, makes for love.

4. NO: Awkwardness is sometimes appealing, and in any case love-making should be unstudied.

5. (d) is correct. Love phrases should not be parroted, as a rule.

6. YES: A good lover is always considerate.

7. YES: (See 6 above.)

8. NO: Monotony can destroy romance.

9. NO: (See 8 above.)

10. YES

11. If you used not more than 5 words, credit yourself 1 point.

12. NO: Stilted or forced behavior handicaps a lover.

181

13. (a) YES, (b) NO, (c) NO. Credit yourself 1 point for each correct answer in this item.

14. YES: A good lover makes it his business to find out what makes his loved one happy.

15. YES: (See 8 above.)

16. YES

17. NO: (See 8 above.)

18. YES

19. (c)

20. NO: If you answered YES, you have difficulty in losing yourself in romance, in giving yourself up completely to love's embrace.

Give yourself 1 point for each correct answer, except where otherwise stated.

SD:3.3   PE:2.3

19. Do People Like You?

1. NO: Even if folks do scrutinize you all day—which they don't, of course—you should ignore it. Self-consciousness makes you stiff, wooden; may tempt you into acting "phoney."

2. NO: It's all right to bore your friends a little (that's what friends are for), but you should know when they have had enough.

3. NO: Preserving dignity at any cost only serves to keep people at a distance. When something comical happens, for instance, it is better to break down and guffaw like everybody else.

4. NO: The worst bore is the person who is always pointing out that you are inconsistent, illogical, mistaken, etc. People have a right to expect a certain amount of indulgence from others, unless the issues are gravely important

5. NO: People are more sensitive than generally realized to another's conscious effort to "put himself across," and are inclined to react unfavorably.

6. YES: It shows interest, and is rather flattering.

7. NO: While the person who allows himself to be the continual butt of jokes is regarded as a poor specimen, the fellow who can't ever "take it" has too brittle an ego to make many friends.

8. NO: For the same reason as in Question 7.

182

9. NO: Often such people want appreciation, rather than a duel of wits. The best rule is to "be yourself."

10. NO: It is part of good fellowship to adjust to the mood of others if not too inconvenient; but if you are *always* careful to do so, you will leave the impression of being a namby-pamby with no individuality.

11. NO: A person should help his friends because he *wants* to help them. Ulterior motives hurt your chances of being liked.

12. NO: To win friends, don't be concerned about whether others appreciate you. Be concerned about whether you appreciate others.

13. YES: The more you give and the less you take, the more popular you are likely to be—despite the arguments of cynics to the contrary.

14. YES: He helps—even though he doesn't expect or demand reciprocation.

15. NO: For the same reason as in Question 5.

16. NO: Better to suffer in silence and let the other fellow have his moment.

17. NO: This is too close to being false and calculating; the forced laugh alienates as many as the superior smile.

18. NO: Frankness shows honesty and at least is respected; whereas a lame excuse is worse than none, for it is liable to be suspect, and at all events is insincere.

19. NO: It is right to try to help, but not to nag; accepting a person as he is, faults and all, pays dividends in affection.

20. YES: The introduction to this test argued that harmful stupidity, foolishness and unreasonableness deserve condemnation. This is not to say that every time someone disagrees with you— especially in matters of little importance—you should ride roughshod over his opinion. Hesitate to hit the other fellow in the ego, where he is most sensitive. True persuasion comes from appreciating the other fellow's point of view.

You get 5 points for each correct answer.

20. Are You Really Happy?

1. NO: Crowds are exhilarating, if anything, to the well adjusted.

2. NO: An affirmative answer shows departure from normal; may indicate fears or anxieties.

3. NO: This may be wise, but unrelieved pessimism disallows the hope and expectation essential to happiness.

4. NO: Unrelieved optimism is abnormal, and will lead to more than a normal share of disappointments.

5. NO: If you feel this way, you may be oversensitive to trivialities or lose larger values for the sake of gaining smaller ones; and neither attitude is conducive to happiness.

6. NO: A person truly enjoying life is usually anxious to "act, act in the living present!".

7. NO: (If you are 16 years old or younger, give yourself credit even if you answer "Yes.") Such daydreams in a mature person may indicate inadequate adjustment to reality, or repressed ambitions, wants impossible to achieve, dissatisfaction with self, etc.

8. NO: If you admit that other elements play a part in success or failure, you save yourself much anguish, self-reproach, frustration.

9. YES: Strong enthusiasms and interests, though occasionally interfering with business or social life, make for a wholesome, healthy attitude—with adequate escape and relief from tension.

10. NO: An affirmative answer hints at least mild social or biological maladjustment, selfconsciousness.

11. NO: Whether or not this is true, if you *think* it is then you show poor adjustment to half the people in the world—a condition not conducive to happiness.

12. NO: Envy, jealousy, destroy happiness. Your attitude should be: No one gets paid too much—it's just that the rest get paid too little.

13. NO: A "yes" here might show a mild form of what is popularly called a "persecution complex."

14. NO: For the reason mentioned in 11.

15. NO: A reasonable conclusion is generally enough to justify

action. Exhaustively weighing all questions is an impossible task; attempting it shows lack of proportion, is a symptom of worry and poor confidence.

16. NO: If you consider yourself sensitive in this regard, it is probably because you are often hurt.

17. (a) YES, (b) YES, (c) YES: Whether or not these statements are correct, a large majority of people *think* they are (in the U. S.) If you depart frequently from the *mores* and beliefs of your times—though you may be correct and courageous in doing so—you run the risk of unhappiness.

If you answered at least one of the three right, credit yourself with one point for the entire question.

18. Faith and its corollary, hope, are essential to happiness. NO to all four queries would indicate lack of capacity for faith. YES to conflicting queries shows confusion and lack of any real faith.

If you answered YES to only one query, give yourself two points for the entire question.

If you answered YES to (a) and (d), give yourself two points for the entire question.

If you answered YES to either (b) and (c) or (c) and (d), give yourself two points for the entire question.

Other answers get no credit.

19. YES: For the reason mentioned in 18.

20. If you answered FALSE *to* (a), TRUE to (b) and FALSE to (c), *credit yourself with two points.*

If you answered TRUE to (a), TRUE to (b) and FALSE to (c), *credit yourself with one point.*

Other answers get no credit.

TO GET YOUR SCORE—Credit yourself with 1 point for each correct answer, except as indicated in Answers 17, 18 and 20.

21. Can You Take It?

1. The letter "Z" in the first line should be crossed out.
2. A cross should appear on the first dotted line.
3. The number "23" should appear on the second dotted line.
4. The number "9" should appear on the third dotted line.

5. "A," "E," "I," "O," should appear on the fifth dotted line.

6. A circle should be drawn around "ZOO" in the first line.

7. A square should appear on the sixth dotted line.

8. "5," "6," "7," "8," "9," "10," should be written on the seventh line, in that order.

9. Your drawing of a ball should appear at the left of the word "draw."

10. A comma should be inserted to make the phrase read THAT THAT IS, IS.

11. "ZOWIE" should be written on the eighth dotted line.

12. A line should be drawn over "a" in "Draw a line........".

13. A line should be drawn under "three" in "Write three words........".

14., 15., 16. *Give yourself 1 point for each word ending in "x" which you have written at the top of the page. If you have written more than three words, don't give yourself any points.*

17. "XYZ" should be written in the left-hand margin.

18. Your age should appear on the last dotted line.

19. "UNCLE" should appear at the end of the last line.

Give yourself 1 point for each correct answer, except as stated below in Answers 14, 15 and 16. Total points is your score.

SD:2   PE:1.4

22. How's Your Judgment?

1—Check "If you cannot answer". 2—Check "If you cannot answer". 3—D. 4—D. 5—B. 6—A.

Give yourself 2 points for each answer omitted or wrongly marked

23. Are You Decisive?

Example I: D, E, G. Example II: C, G, H. Example III: C, G, H. Example IV: 5, 7, 9. Example V: 2, 3. *Score yourself 3 points for each wrong answer, 10 points for each failure to make the full number of checks per example as specified in the directions.*

SD:12:7   PE:8.6

24. Are You Thorough?

(1)15, (2)12, (3)18, (4)6, (5)2, (6)5, (7)5, (8)4, (9)4, (10)1

Score yourself 2 points for each wrongly answered question, and 1 point for each unanswered question. Add these points for your total score.

25. Test Your Marriage!

1. FALSE: This attitude might prevent the all-out, hell-or-high-water effort of a marriage partner to overcome the difficulties which sometimes threaten wedlock.

2. FALSE: While similar interests often hold a marriage together many happy marriages are on record which show complete dissimilarity of tastes and interests on the part of husband and wife. Indeed, similar interests can be dangerous, leading to boredom or even to unpleasant rivalry—as with male and female bridge experts, say, who decide to get married.

3. FALSE: It helps, but people with a talent for marriage can do without it.

4. FALSE: An affirmative answer may indicate a type of ignorance or insufficiency dangerous to married happiness.

5. FALSE: It is bound to change, perhaps, but not necessarily to weaken.

6. FALSE

7. FALSE: Deep friendship can be the strongest bond between man and wife.

8. FALSE: What of the aged? Such attraction often fades to a large degree, to be replaced by dependence, respect, friendship, mutual need and similar welding forces.

9. FALSE: Routine and lack of spontaneity are fatal.

10. TRUE: Apart from the moral side of this question, statistical indications are that such dalliance affords a safety valve for pressures which might otherwise explode a marriage.

11. FALSE

12. FALSE: Here again occurs the danger of routine. For happy marriage, a couple should indulge when the spirit moves them.

13. FALSE: As statistics show.

14. FALSE

187

15. FALSE: It may be that a person can indeed deeply love two members of the opposite sex simultaneously. To believe this, however, is a dangerous attitude for a married person.

16. FALSE: Some degree of social activity is essential to a healthy marriage.

17. FALSE: See answer to Question 16.

18. FALSE: Too light an attitude toward love may weaken the marriage vows.

19. FALSE: It has its lighter side.

20. FALSE: It helps—but some terrible cooks have made excellent wives.

21. FALSE: Occasionally a vacation *from* each other is a big help.

22. TRUE: See answer to Question 21.

23. (c.) is the correct answer. That is, it reveals the attitude most conducive to happy marriage.

24. FALSE: A sharing of all that matters is generally the surest mark of a happy marriage.

25. FALSE: Such a situation will not destroy a marriage unless the basic conditions of marital happiness were not present in the first place.

Give yourself 1 point for each correct answer. Total points is your score.

26. Can You Handle People?

Maybe you can handle people, but are too rash—or too hesitant— in making choices under time pressure. If so, it hints that you might not be fully effective in a broad range of managerial and executive capacities—and so your score is penalized.

1. (A), 2. (A), 3. (A) Both your appreciation and your priority should be mentioned to the employee. 4. (left) (smaller) (right), 5. (C), 6. (A), 7. (B), 8. (B), 9. (B), 10. (B)

Give yourself 3 points for each correct answer.

Subtract 5 points if you made more than two "no choice" answers.

Subtract 5 points if you did not make any "no choice" answers. (If you answered question 5 correctly, it will count as one of the "no choice" answers.)

Subtract 3 points for each unanswered question.

27. Can You Assess Situations?

Despite the title, this is a test for certain attitudes which, whether we like it or not, appear to characterize a majority of "successful" business executives. For purposes of this test, "success" has two criteria: first, a minimum salary of twelve thousand dollars annually —and second, superior effectiveness on the job, as judged by fellow executives. The factors involved seem to add up to a kind of armor against moral or ethical criticism, the avoidance of quibble, and emphasis on ends rather than means.

1. TRUE, 2. FALSE, 3. TRUE, 4. TRUE, 5. FALSE, 6. FALSE, 7. FALSE, 8. TRUE, 9. FALSE, 10, TRUE, 11. TRUE, 12.FALSE

Score yourself 2 points for each wrongly answered question, and 1 point for each unanswered question. Add these points for your total score.

28. Are You Ingenious?

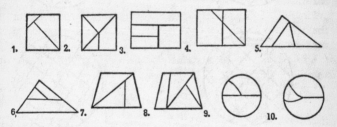

Score yourself 2 points for each correct answer. Subtract 1 point for each unanswered question.

29. Have You A Mechanical Bent?

1-b, 2-a, 3-b, 4-a, 5-b, 6-b, 7-c, 8-c, 9-d, 10-c (the nut can be turned by striking its edge with the hammer), 11-c, 12-b (The next step would be to build another mound of stones or dirt under the rear axle. You can then kick the spare tire free, and the flat will be high enough from the ground for you to remove it). 13-c, 14-c.

Give yourself 5 points for each correct answer.

A: KNACK FOR HANDLING TOOLS—*Add the above score to your scores in 29.* Have You Motor Ability? *and 30.* Are You Dextrous?

SD:35   PE:23.6

B: MECHANICAL UNDERSTANDING—*Add the above score to your scores in 11.* Can You Visualize? *and 12.* Are You Inventive?

SD:28.7   PE:19.4

30. Have You Pattern Skill?

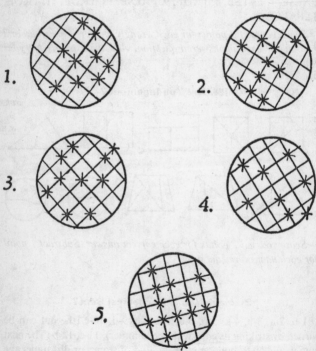

Give yourself 2 points for each X you placed properly according to the diagrams above.

SD:8.7   PE:5.9

31. Have You Motor Ability?

PART ONE:

Give yourself 1 point for each dot you made anywhere on this page.

PART TWO:

Give yourself 2 points for each dot within a circle.

For your score, add all points in both parts, then divide by 10.

SD:16.5   PE:11

32. Are You Dextrous?

PART ONE:

Give yourself 1 point for each properly marked square or circle. If your dot is outside the square, or if any part of your X crosses the circumference of the circle, you get no credit.

PART TWO:

Give yourself 6 points for each line properly marked.

To find your score total the points you received in both parts then divide this total by 2.

SD:10   PE:6.9

A SELECTION OF NON-FICTION TITLES
AVAILABLE FROM CORGI BOOKS

☐ 13421 X	THE BULLSEYE QUIZ BOOK		£2.50
☐ 12299 8	THE FURTHER PROPHECIES OF NOSTRADAMUS		
		Erika Cheetham	£2.99
☐ 12272 8	KNOW YOUR OWN PSI-Q	Eysenck & Sargent	£2.50
☐ 12555 5	IN SEARCH OF SCHRODINGER'S CAT	John Gribbin	£4.99
☐ 12656 X	IN SEARCH OF THE DOUBLE HELIX	John Gribbin	£4.95
☐ 13146 6	IN SEARCH OF THE BIG BANG	John Gribbin	£5.99
☐ 98051 X	THE COMPLETE BOOK OF SELF-SUFFICIENCY	John Seymour	£12.95
☐ 98013 7	IRELAND: A TERRIBLE BEAUTY	Jill and Leon Uris	£9.75
☐ 12623 3	THE RIGHT BRAIN EXPERIENCE	Marilee Zdenek	£5.99